The Police on the Urban Frontier

A Guide to Community Understanding

By **GEORGE EDWARDS**
Judge, U.S. Court of Appeals
FOR THE SIXTH CIRCUIT
Police Commissioner of Detroit, 1962-63

Foreword by Ramsey Clark
Attorney General of the U.S.

INSTITUTE OF HUMAN RELATIONS PRESS
The American Jewish Committee
165 East 56 Street, New York, N.Y. 10022

Designed by JOAN HANSCH

Edited and produced
by the PUBLICATIONS SERVICE
of the AMERICAN JEWISH COMMITTEE
SONYA F. KAUFER, *Director*

Copyright © 1968 THE AMERICAN JEWISH COMMITTEE
All rights reserved
Printed in the United States of America

About the Author

THE HON. GEORGE EDWARDS was Police Commissioner of Detroit in 1962-63 and is now a Judge of the United States Court of Appeals for the Sixth Circuit. In preceding years he has also been a Justice of the Supreme Court of Michigan; Circuit Judge of the Third Judicial Circuit, Wayne County, Michigan; Probate Judge in charge of the Wayne County Juvenile Court; President of the Detroit Common Council; Director-Secretary of the Detroit Housing Commission; and Director of the Welfare Department of the United Automobile Workers (CIO).

Judge Edwards was appointed by the Chief Justice of the United States to head the Committee on the Administration of the Criminal Law of the Judicial Conference of the United States — the governing body for the administration of the Federal judicial system as a whole. He is a member of the Council of Judges of the National Council on Crime and Delinquency, and of the National Commission on the Reform of the Federal Criminal Law.

Acknowledgments

This monograph was inspired by the response to an address delivered by the writer to the United States Conference of Mayors and published in the *Michigan Law Review* (November 1965). Calvin Kytle, William J. Brennan, Jr., and the late Joseph Ross first suggested the expansion of that speech into a handbook for the police and the community.

Vincent Piersante, Horace Gilmore, the Rev. Hubert Locke and Vincent Broderick read and commented upon the first draft. None, needless to say, is responsible for the opinions expressed here. Particular assistance and encouragement also came from Dr. John Dorsey, Arnold Sagalyn, John Doar, Longworth Quinn and Agnes Ingles. Three staff members of the American Jewish Committee — Harry Fleischman, Sonya Kaufer and George Salomon — gave invaluable editorial assistance. Margaret Edwards read and helped edit all the drafts and, even more important, shared with me the fascinating experience of our urban frontier.

Contents

Introduction	1
The Police in the 20th-Century City	4
The Challenge to Law Enforcement	6
The Conflict Between Negroes and Police	24
19th-Century Tools for 20th-Century Tasks	34
Recommendations in Brief	38
Police Professionalization	41
The Disciplined Use of Force	48
More — and More Effective — Law Enforcement	55
Effective Race Riot Control	58
Channels of Communication	69
Organizing Citizen Support	77
Toward a 20th-Century Police Force	86

As a law enforcement officer, my fundamental duty is to serve mankind; to safeguard lives and property; to protect the innocent against deception, the weak against oppression or intimidation, and the peaceful against violence or disorder; and to respect the Constitutional rights of all men to liberty, equality and justice.... I will never act officiously or permit personal feelings, prejudices, animosities or friendships to influence my decisions. With no compromise for crime and with relentless prosecution of criminals, I will enforce the law courteously and appropriately without fear or favor, malice or ill will, never employing unnecessary force or violence....
— Police Officers' Code of Ethics

... Asked about charges of police brutality he [Los Angeles Chief of Police William H. Parker] answered flatly, "There is no brutality." And when the riot did get reasonably under control [he said:] "We're on top and they are on the bottom." That, in a nutshell, is the heart of the Negroes' complaint: they claim it has been ever thus.
— Report on the Watts riot, by Don Moser
Life, August 27, 1965

The abrasive relationship between the police and the ghetto community has been a major — and explosive — source of grievance, tension and disorder. The blame must be shared by the total society. . . . Police administrators, with the guidance of public officials, and the support of the entire community, must take vigorous action to improve law enforcement and to decrease the potential for disorder.
— National Advisory Commission on Civil Disorders, February 29, 1968

They who make peaceful revolution impossible make violent revolution inevitable. — President John F. Kennedy

FOREWORD

by RAMSEY CLARK
Attorney General of the United States

CHANGE IS the fundamental fact of our time. Scientific advance doubles our knowledge of the physical world each decade. Who among the 76 million Americans in 1900 dreamed of television, or 80 million automobiles or the supersonic air transport which is nearly upon us? In 1900 our people were largely rural, now we are 80 per cent urban, and living in cities of 50,000 or more.

No one has experienced greater change than the Negro. More rural in 1900 than our people as a whole, he is more urban today, and also the most migrant and anonymous. Eric Hoffer has said, "... When a population undergoing drastic change is without abundant opportunities for individual action and self-advancement, it develops a hunger for faith, pride and unity. . . . We are told that revolutions are set in motion to realize radical changes. Actually it is drastic change which sets the stage for revolution. . . ."

When in history has there been turbulence within a nation that the poor were not in turmoil? Today, when the poor are a small minority in our country, it may be more difficult than ever for them to be resigned, both because they are a minority, and because television and magazines portray the affluence which surrounds them in the very midst of the poverty and misery in which they live.

But for all the change we have experienced and the frustrations and anger generated, the overwhelming majority of our people in all sections of the country and all parts of every city, of all ages and races and religions, believe in these United States, believe in order under law, know our purposes are just and have faith that we will attain equal justice.

An immense and growing effort is underway: to rebuild cities, to educate all our people, to give every American the chance to live where he wants, to do whatever his abilities and energies make possible for him. We are only beginning in these last several years, but we can clearly succeed, if we have time.

Whether we have the time needed will depend more on the policeman than on anyone else. This is why the policeman is the most important American in 1968. He works in a highly flammable environment. A spark can cause an explosion. He must maintain order without provocation which will cause combustion.

The need is for balance, firmness without fear, a careful control with minimum friction. He must be fair. He cannot be repressive. If he overacts, he can cause a riot. If he underacts, he can permit a riot.

Police-community relations is the most important law enforcement problem of today and the years ahead. As never before, the policeman needs full community support. And as never before, the community needs him.

Every officer must be a community relations expert. He must serve the public, and the public must respect, support and compensate him for the vital role he plays.

Police-community relations is a two-way street. The community must work for it as hard as the police. It is both ironic and tragic that we have given so little to the support of those on whom so much depends. Underpaid, undertrained, and overworked, they are called on to perform hard, unpleasant and dangerous work, all too frequently midst suspicion and hostility.

It is imperative that we strive now to professionalize all our local police. Substantial salary increases are essential; higher standards and vigorous and continuing training a must. Most of all we must integrate the policeman into our total community life and give that respect and status deserved by him on whom both liberty and safety chiefly depend.

If the policeman succeeds in his assignment, we shall have a chance in ours.

The pages that follow offer a guide to both the police and the community in pursuance of the goals common to us all. I commend them to concerned citizens everywhere.

AUTHOR'S PREFACE

THE WRITING of this pamphlet in the midst of the greatest civil strife in the United States since the end of the Civil War is at best a risky undertaking. History is so much easier to analyze a decade after the event than amid the turmoil and conflict of the event itself. And history has a way of sweeping aside both program and prophecy by producing what was never thought of, or what was deemed impossible. Also, many will feel that to attempt a critical analysis of the role of police in the United States, at a time when society relies principally upon police for protection, is little short of treasonable. At least this is likely to be the view of the John Birch Society, whose slogan, "Support your local police," has become a call for wholly unthinking and uncritical support.

As will become apparent, we by no means underestimate the danger to which racial extremists can subject our already vulnerable cities by exploiting the Negro community's resentment over intolerable social conditions. Newark and Detroit may indeed only be prologue to tragedies to come. But if, as we think, American police forces are impossibly ill-equipped in numbers, training, weaponry and program, and often in attitudes, to deal with the problems of this year and years to come, then the time to say so is now — while something might yet be done.

The twin problems of this decade are to complete the civil rights revolution and, by lawful methods, to keep terrorists from destroying American society.

If we fail to do the former, we may betray American democracy and find ourselves moving toward apartheid and a Fascist state.

If we fail to do the latter, we may risk the destruction of our cities and the anarchy of civil war.

The time of decision is now!

G.E.

March 1968

INTRODUCTION

A RIVER of hate runs through the dark streets of the central areas in our cities. Those who live and work there, whether black or white, are washed continually by its bitter waters.

Race prejudice is two-sided; it is deep; and it is explosive. There is no such thing as a controlled race riot. Once racial violence runs loose on city streets, fear and hatred tend to turn human beings, white and black, into savages. Usually, utterly innocent people are the victims.

In one of the major riots of this century, race hatred took over the streets of a great city for 24 bloody hours. Thirty-six people died. One was a doctor who had practiced medicine on the east side of the city for many years. He was white, of Italian origin, but had many Negro patients. The morning the riot broke out, he was called by one of these patients, and promptly set out to visit him. On the street, he was met by a mob full of anger and race hatred. They didn't know the doctor; all they knew was that they had black faces and his was white. The mob stoned him to death.[1]

Later in that same 24-hour period, a Negro workman was heading home from his job, driving alone. He was stopped by a mob full of anger and race hatred. They knew nothing about him except that his face was black and theirs were white. They turned his car

---

1. The victim was Dr. Joseph De Horatiis, who was killed June 21, 1943. See Robert Shogan and Tom Craig, *The Detroit Race Riot* (Philadelphia: Chilton Books, 1964), pp. 2, 51. This version of Dr. De Horatiis' death is based in part upon the original Detroit Police Department record pertaining to the case.

over, set fire to the gas tank, and burned him to death in the car.[2]

During the last few summers, America has seen tragedies of the same kind enacted in almost all of its large cities. In 1960, James Baldwin's essay, *The Fire Next Time*, warned of coming explosions; beginning in 1964, the prediction came to pass — more devastatingly each year — with the "Burn, baby, burn" incendiarism of Philadelphia, Watts, New York, Newark, Detroit, and other large urban centers.

All of these disasters have had one conspicuous feature in common: each was triggered by a confrontation between a Negro citizen and a policeman.

The relationship between the police and minority groups in big-city ghettos is one of the sorest spots in American life today. In the words of a recent report by the President's Commission on Law Enforcement and Administration of Justice, a "wall of isolation" surrounds the police, blocking understanding between them and the dwellers in the slums, and permitting the growth of every kind of misunderstanding and hatred. And the even more recent report of the President's National Advisory Commission on Civil Disorders urges drastic changes in police operations to stem rising militancy and estrangement between whites and Negroes.

The policeman, whose mission it is to guard the peace, walks uneasily in the ghetto. What worries him is not so much the ordinary criminal; usually he feels he can cope with lawbreakers, whose apprehension is his main job. He fears, rather, the very people he is there to protect. For many otherwise law-abiding ghetto dwellers are openly hostile to him; many refuse to cooperate with him in maintaining law and order; and on occasion some may attack him.

Ghetto residents for their part complain of mistreatment by police. In every major city, police brutality is a familiar com-

---

2. This is one of a number of unidentified deaths which occurred during the Detroit riot of 1943. The story as given here was related to the author, then a member of the Detroit City Council, by the Battalion Commander of the Detroit Fire Department, which reported to the scene and investigated the episode.

plaint — on picket signs, at police stations, in hearings at City Hall. And this charge cannot be dismissed as empty talk by irresponsible elements; it has been effectively documented by three authoritative national commissions over a period of four decades,[3] and is a matter of deep concern to many sensible, law-abiding citizens, both Negroes and whites.

Yet the nation, by and large, has failed to take effective action against this mutual hostility, which figures so large in what may prove to be America's gravest domestic crisis since the Civil War. We have voiced our support of the police in their job of quelling disorders, on the grounds that, whatever the causes of unrest, order must prevail. But where the equally urgent task of reconciling the underlying conflict is concerned, our efforts usually have been "too little and too late." Thus, in 1967, virtually all large cities were stepping up police planning and training for riot control; few were working effectively on police-community programs to lessen tensions.

If this conflict is to be resolved without even graver catastrophes, every big city must step up its efforts to remedy what is wrong with its police practices — to provide equal and effective law enforcement, and to make racial confrontations as bloodless as possible. The nation as a whole must devise and support a comprehensive program for increasing the professional caliber and the effectiveness of local police forces. And citizens, individually or through their organizations, must back and assist these efforts at every level. We will not have first-rate law enforcement until the people make it a truly national concern.

---

3. National Commission on Law Observance and Enforcement [Wickersham Commission], *Report on Lawlessness in Law Enforcement* (Washington: U. S. Government Printing Office, 1931); President's Commission on Civil Rights, *To Secure These Rights* (New York: Simon & Schuster, 1947); *The 50 States Report*, submitted to the Commission on Civil Rights by the State Advisory Committees, 1961 (Washington: U. S. Government Printing Office, 1961).

THE POLICE IN THE 20th-CENTURY CITY

IN MODERN America, an effective police force is vastly more important than it was in former times. As our civilization has changed from rural to urban, we have turned over more and more of its burdens to the police — far more than most people recognize. Today, police officers determine, to no small degree, the safety and quality of city life. How they do their job may well decide whether or not the city as we know it will survive.

The policemen who patrol the streets of our cities have to deal not only with overeager drivers, drunks, thieves and muggers, but also with unruly or abandoned children, bickering adults and disturbed persons. What is more, we ask them to handle all of the tasks they encounter — from accidents and violent crimes to personal problems that were once thought to be private family affairs — with the wisdom of a Solomon, the concern of a social worker and the prompt courage of a combat soldier.

Here is a sampling of the problems which the police in cities must cope with:

- A car runs out of gas in the middle of a crowded expressway.
- A child is impaled on a steel reinforcing rod in a building excavation.
- An 11-year-old boy is found wandering on the street at 2 o'clock in the morning.
- A mentally retarded youngster is suspected of setting fires in his neighborhood.
- A bookie is using a complex electronic device, called a "cheese box," to conceal his telephone number.
- Boys are playing ball in the streets, and the neighbors complain. (If the police chase the boys off the streets, where do they go?)

— A young man assaults his father, who calls the police. (But when the police subdue him, the father attacks them for abusing his son.)
— A motorist has to be removed from the tangled wreckage of a head-on collision.
— Black nationalists are holding an angry street meeting in the heat of summer, in the city's most crowded neighborhood.
— A pregnant woman cannot reach the hospital in time, and her baby must be delivered in the back seat of a scout car.

The police radio — the control center of every metropolitan police department — is where these and all other tasks of the force converge. A citizen calls for help, usually by telephone. At once, a police dispatcher calls the nearest scout car with the address of the "run" and a description of the trouble, phrased in terse, lean English that tells the story fast. A citizen will report a drunk lying unconscious on the curb at Van Dyke and Jefferson Streets. That goes over the police radio as "Car 92: Jefferson and Van Dyke, one down." Or someone may complain that his neighbors are shouting and coming to blows — over disciplining the children, say, or too much drinking, or a new dress she wants, or a party where he paid too much attention to another woman. The police radio sums it up: "17201 Tournelle, family trouble." If a weapon figures in the altercation, a warning is added.

The officer in the scout car promptly answers "Got it," and the tone in which he says it sometimes tells volumes. If a bandit with a revolver is reported to be holding up a drugstore, the words are spat out with assurance and urgency; here the officer is headed for a tense combat situation for which he is trained and where the lines are clearly drawn. But if it is a case of family trouble, the words are likely to be spoken with weary resignation, as if to say, "Oh, God, here we go again."

Thus, every minute of the day and night, the police radio voices the toils and troubles of the city — as well as the toils and troubles of the police in their responses to the city's problems. And when the parable of the good Samaritan is reenacted in the streets of our 20th-century cities, the Samaritan more often than not wears a blue coat.

THE CHALLENGE TO LAW ENFORCEMENT

YET THE police function is in trouble in every section of the United States. New needs and responsibilities in law enforcement are multiplying, as a result of six major trends in American life:

1. The increase in urban crime.
2. The effects of urbanization.
3. The impact of population migration.
4. The United States Supreme Court's requirement of police compliance with the Bill of Rights.
5. The impact of the civil rights movement.
6. The rising tide of race riots and violence.

It is easy to understand why these trends exist, and to find justification for all but the first and the last. But the fact remains that each in some way has compounded the problems of local police and contributed to the current crisis in law enforcement.

The Increase in Urban Crime

Almost any day, in almost any part of the country, a glance at the newspaper will leave one with the impression that America is living amid a staggering increase in all forms of lawlessness — a crime wave inundating our cities and overwhelming the police. Taken at face value, the statistics seem to bear out this view. In 1965, 2,780,015 "offenses known to the police" were recorded by the FBI's uniform crime index: recorded crimes against property were up 35 per cent since 1960, and recorded crimes against persons were up 25 per cent. If we adjust these figures for population growth, we are still left with an increase.

Actually, the matter is not so clear-cut. As a careful, not at all alarmist report of the National Crime Commission points out, the uniform crime index is a highly fallible resource in tracing crime trends, for there is not always the same amount (though always a vast amount) of *unreported* crime. Much of the increase in recorded offenses may simply be a result of more accurate or more honest police reporting, and of the greater willingness of some people to tell the police about unlawful acts. Another part of the increase is doubtless due to large-scale migration from jurisdictions where most offenses weren't recorded to where they are. Some increase in crime reporting is simply due to broader insurance coverage, which naturally stimulates reporting of violations. Each of these factors could cause an increase in reported offenses, quite independent of any actual rise in crime.

Even so, the National Crime Commission concluded: "There is much crime in America, more than ever is reported, far more than ever is solved, far too much for the health of the Nation.[4] . . . The existence of crime, the talk about crime, the reports of crime, and the fear of crime have eroded the basic quality of life of many Americans."[5] And, whether the increase in reported crime is real or statistical, whether it reflects declining moral values or higher standards of law enforcement, it places added demands upon an already burdened police force.

Urbanization

At the turn of this century, America was still overwhelmingly a rural nation. Today, for better or worse, the great majority of our people live in cities. This rapid urbanization is closely linked with the high incidence of crime. As Plutarch observed nearly 2,000 years ago, "the city is the teacher of the man." But the city teaches both good and evil.

The city's complexity and congestion greatly increase the chances

---

4. *The Challenge of Crime in a Free Society: A Report by the President's Commission on Law Enforcement and Administration of Justice* (Washington: February 1967), p. 1.

5. *Ibid.*, Summary, page v.

of disturbance and crime. Sheer lack of space heightens the chances of property damage; overcrowding (particularly the inhuman overcrowding of the slums) produces explosions of youthful energy and, with them, conflict. The frustrations of tenement living lead readily to fights, to alcoholism, to drug addiction and to assaults and murder.

At the same time, the anonymity of the city creates license. In big-city street crimes, there is almost always someone who has seen what happened; but the witness probably knows neither victim nor assailant, and may not even be sure which is which. Often he will not feel sufficiently concerned with the affair to call the police. Meanwhile, actual or potential criminals know that in the city they can escape the eye and control of families and acquaintances.

Furthermore, opportunities for crime are greatest in the city. On the farm, some property, such as poultry or livestock, is likely to be closely held and defended. Other kinds of property, like fruit in season, may be available in abundance, and no one will care much if a little is taken. But the self-service supermarket and the $3,000 automobile with the keys in place are temptations of the city. It is not improbable that the same temptations that led another generation to steal apples now lead to shoplifting and automobile theft.

Finally, the big city puts affluence and the worst poverty side by side. And television or the movies constantly bring reminders of unattainable wants into the hearts of slum dwellers.

No wonder, then, that high crime rates are primarily an urban phenomenon. In 1965, according to the *Uniform Crime Reports*, cities with populations over 1,000,000 had the highest rate of known offenses for five of the seven index crimes: homicide, forcible rape, robbery, aggravated assault and larceny. The highest rates for the other two — burglary and motor-vehicle theft — were found in cities from 250,000 to 1,000,000.

The National Crime Commission reports that of 2,780,015 "offenses known to the police" in 1965, some 2 million occurred in cities, more than half a million in suburbs, and only about 170,000 in rural areas. The number of crimes per 100,000 residents was over 1,800 in cities, just under 1,200 in suburbs, and 617 in the country. If we assume that there has been an actual, not just a statistical, increase in crime, these figures strongly suggest that urbanization is one basic cause.

In almost every way, law enforcement is a larger and more complex job in an urban than in a rural setting. When a farm boy on a spring day, a generation ago, yelled, ran, picked up a rock and threw it — who cared? He was a boy. But when a city boy of today, moved by the same animal spirits, throws rocks, he is likely to set off a police call and find himself a police statistic.

Freedom on the frontier is one thing; freedom in the metropolis is another. On the frontier, liberty meant simply the right of each man to do without hindrance almost anything he wanted to do; but in the big city, liberty might be better defined as the maximum freedom of choice that can be given each man without trespassing on the freedom of others. People in Daniel Boone's time would not have put up with traffic lights; they needed none on their foot trails. But we accept traffic lights, even though they interfere with our liberty, because we know that without them all of us would be constantly snarled in hopeless traffic jams.

The basic job of every organized government from the beginning of history has been to keep order. But the United States, throughout its history, has looked upon liberty as an equally sacred objective. The policeman has to reconcile the two, and in the big city that can be quite a task.

Migration

Of the various aspects of urbanization, the one that has had far and away the greatest impact upon problems of law enforcement has been the migration of millions from the rural South to the core areas of the great Northern cities. Some of these newcomers, particularly in Midwestern centers, are white "hillbillies"; but the overwhelming majority are Negroes.

The significance of the Negro migration can be pictured to some degree even from the bare statistics. Senator Robert F. Kennedy, in a recent speech, cited the following figures:

In 1910 only 29 percent of American Negroes lived in urban areas. Then the great migration began. By 1960, 65 percent lived in urban areas.

And of the Negroes who lived in urban areas in 1960, 80 percent were concentrated in the central cities.

Between 1950 and 1960 alone, the number of Negroes in the central cities increased by 3¼ million....

Nearly every major city has within it one or more large areas where the population is more than 95 percent Negro. One area in Chicago of nearly 350,000 is 97.9 percent Negro. Central Harlem, an area of over 241,000 people, is also 97.9 percent Negro.[6]

It has often been pointed out that this is by no means the first wave of migration which the great American cities have been required to absorb. They received and educated the millions of immigrants who arrived from European countries in the decades immediately before and after 1900. Today, the variety of names found in every important segment of American life testifies to the cities' capacity for assimilating masses of poor immigrants.

To date, the Negro migration has proved a harder problem. Charles E. Silberman notes that between 1950 and 1960 the 12 largest cities gained nearly two million poor Negro residents, while losing over two million white middle-class residents to the suburbs. The cities, he says, are in trouble because they are not dealing successfully with the newcomers from Mississippi or Tennessee, as they once did with those from County Cork or Sicily:

> It is the explosive growth of their Negro populations ... that constitutes the large cities' principal problems and concern. When city officials talk about spreading slums, they are talking in the main about physical deterioration of the areas inhabited by Negroes. And when they talk about juvenile delinquency, or the burden of welfare payments, or any of a long list of city problems, officials are talking principally about the problems of Negro adjustment to city life. For the large city is not absorbing and "urbanizing" its new Negro residents rapidly enough; its slums are no longer acting as the incubator of a new middle class.[7]

---

6. *Congressional Record*, February 2, 1966, pp. 1787-1788.
7. Charles E. Silberman, "The City and the Negro," *Fortune*, March 1962, pp. 88-91, 139-154.

In 1961, James B. Conant, with unhappy prophecy, warned of the "social dynamite" which this unassimilated migration was piling up in the cities:

> In a slum section, composed almost entirely of Negroes, in one of our largest cities, 59 per cent of the male youth between 16 and 21 were out of school and unemployed. They were roaming the streets. . . . In another city, in a slum area of 125,000 people, mostly Negro, a sampling indicated that roughly 70 per cent of the boys and girls aged 16 to 21 were unemployed. When one stops to consider that the total population of this district is equal to that of a good-sized independent city, the magnitude of the problem is appalling and the challenge to our society is clear. . . .[8]

High-school graduation, Dr. Conant continued, does not necessarily improve young Negroes' job chances very much: In one Negro slum, two-thirds of male high-school dropouts were found to be without jobs, but so were roughly half of the graduates. "The unemployed floaters . . . are walking evidence that the door of the neighborhood schoolhouse opens on a dead-end street."

To talk of delinquencies committed by Negroes, or to describe the children of Negro migrants as "social dynamite" in our cities, may seem to give ammunition to those who claim that Negro citizens of this country are essentially a "criminal class." Anyone who looks at the facts must reject such a notion. While it is true that in most of our large cities Negroes commit proportionately more recorded crimes than do whites, the difference is not due to any racial characteristic. Disadvantaged persons of all races have a higher crime rate than the well-off, and Negroes in disproportionate numbers are disadvantaged. Proportionately, far more Negro than white citizens live in slums or congested quarters or both. (In Chicago, proportionately four times as many Negro as white families live under crowded conditions.) Far more hold jobs in the lowest-paid categories; far more are unemployed; far more are school dropouts — and all are members of families which have

---

8. James B. Conant, "Social Dynamite in Our Large Cities." Quoted in: *Social Dynamite*, Report of the Conference on Unemployed, Out-of-School Youth in Urban Areas, May 24-26, 1961 (Washington: National Committee for Children and Youth, 1961), p. 3.

memories of continuous degradation and discrimination through the past 300 years.

All migrants to our country have brought with them both assets and disabilities from their former homes. Negroes bring strength, patience, humor, talent in many of the arts, stoicism in the face of adversity, and an abiding faith in the American dream. But they also bring the bitter heritage of their history.

Nowhere are these scars more evident than in the widespread disorganization of Negro family life. Until slavery ended, just a century ago, marriage was a forbidden institution to the overwhelming majority of Negroes; slave stock was bred by plantation owners as farmers today breed animals. This fact deserves to be borne in mind by critics of Negro divorce and illegitimacy rates. It also should be remembered by those concerned with delinquents, for there is a direct correlation between the incidence of broken homes and that of juvenile delinquency.

Another disadvantage of many of the newcomers to the cities is that they come from areas with no firm tradition of effective law enforcement. In the early part of this century, police in Southern cities tended to shrug off crimes by Negroes against other Negroes. Even in murder cases there was often little or no effort to identify or prosecute the assailant. Property crimes in Negro neighborhoods were largely unreported — or, if reported, ignored. As a result, many Negroes never came to look upon the policeman as the guardian of their own safety and property.

What this adds up to is that crime is not a race problem but is produced by human degradation. If you subject *any* population group, whatever its national origin or color, to poverty, discrimination, denial of rights, lack of education, lack of culture and lack of employment opportunities, that group will produce more than an average percentage of delinquents and criminals. On the other hand, where these disadvantages are not present, Negroes are as law-abiding as whites. In many cities there are long-established neighborhoods where Negro businessmen, lawyers, doctors, or high-seniority factory workers have bought land, built homes and reared their youngsters. Such areas are frequently among the quietest in an entire city. Just as it is easy to police the better white neighborhoods of any city, so it is easy to police the better Negro sections.

The Supreme Court and the Bill of Rights

Over and above the problems posed by shifting social conditions — particularly by the changing status of the Negro — police forces today face increasingly stringent rules in law enforcement.

For over a decade, the Supreme Court has actively led this country toward fuller realization of the high ideals embodied in the Constitution. Article III of the Constitution in effect makes the Supreme Court the interpreter of these ideals; and the present Court has taken that obligation seriously, setting ever higher standards of due process of law.

The Supreme Court has declared, in essence, that only the courts can decide to deprive a person of liberty. In the absence of a judicial warrant or probable cause, there cannot be a lawful arrest; and illegal detention for "investigation" may invalidate an otherwise legal confession.[9]

The Court has reminded us that it is a fundamental principle under our Constitution that a person may not be compelled to testify against himself.[10]

The Court has ruled that when a person is being questioned in police custody after arrest for a crime, he must be informed of his constitutional right to counsel and his right not to testify against himself. Absence of such warnings will result in making a confession inadmissible.[11]

The Court has told us that the Fourth Amendment prohibition of "unreasonable searches and seizures" will be enforced — even against convictions based on procedures that are held consistent with state law.[12]

---

9. *Mallory* v. *U.S.*, 354 U.S. 449 (1957); *McNabb* v. *U.S.*, 318 U.S. 332 (1943).
10. *Leyra* v. *Denno*, 347 U.S. 556 (1954).
11. *Miranda* v. *Arizona*, 384 U.S. 436 (1966).
12. *Mapp* v. *Ohio*, 367 U.S. 643 (1961).

The Court has acted to preserve a defendant's right to be confronted by an accuser and to cross-examine him effectively.[13]

And the Court has held that the Sixth Amendment and the due process clause of the Fourteenth Amendment give indigent defendants, who cannot afford lawyers of their own, a right to counsel at least in all felony prosecutions, whether state or Federal.[14]

These principles do not sound particularly shocking. We are fully familiar with all of them, and we unhesitatingly subscribe to them in theory. But when we do not like the way they affect a specific case — when someone we think guilty is retried or freed because constitutional principle has been disregarded or violated — we become concerned.

Let us then look at the four cases which have occasioned most of the current controversy over the United States Supreme Court: *Mallory, Mapp, Gideon* and *Miranda*.[15]

In the *Mallory* case, a defendant was tried for rape and sentenced to death. He had been detained from early afternoon until the next morning at police headquarters without being taken before a committing magistrate, although such magistrates were available nearby. He was not told of his right to such an arraignment, his right to counsel, or his right to keep silent. By the time he was arraigned, he had made a confession, which figured in the evidence by which he was convicted.

In unanimously reversing the conviction, the Supreme Court stressed that arresting officers could not be left free to depart from the rule of prompt arraignment:

> We cannot sanction this extended delay, resulting in confession, without subordinating the general rule of prompt arraignment to the discretion of arresting officers in finding exceptional circumstances for its disregard.[16]

The Court spelled out the reasons for the rule that the police must promptly show legal cause for arrests:

---

13. *Jencks* v. *U.S.*, 353 U.S. 657 (1947); *Pointer* v. *Texas*, 380 U.S. 400 (1965).
14. *Gideon* v. *Wainwright*, 372 U.S. 335 (1963).
15. See notes 9, 11, 12 and 14.
16. *Mallory* v. *U.S., supra*, 354 U.S. at 455.

... The awful instruments of the criminal law cannot be entrusted to a single functionary. The complicated process of criminal justice is therefore divided into different parts, responsibility for which is separately vested in the various participants upon whom the criminal law relies for its vindication. Legislation such as this, requiring that the police must with reasonable promptness show legal cause for detaining arrested persons, constitutes an important safeguard—not only in assuring protection for the innocent but also in securing conviction of the guilty by methods that commend themselves to a progressive and self-confident society. For this procedural requirement checks resort to those reprehensible practices known as the "third degree" which, through universally rejected as indefensible, still find their way into use. It aims to avoid all the evil implications of secret interrogation of persons accused of crime.[17]

In the *Mapp* case, the defendant was convicted of possessing lewd and lascivious pictures and books. She had refused to admit the police, who had then entered her home forcibly. No search warrant was produced at the trial, nor was the failure to produce one explained. The Ohio Supreme Court upheld the conviction even while considering it to have been "based primarily upon . . . evidence . . . unlawfully seized during an unlawful search of the defendant's home." The U. S. Supreme Court reversed this ruling and held that "all evidence obtained by searches and seizures in violation of the Constitution is, by the same authority, inadmissible in a state court."[18]

In the *Gideon* case, the defendant was charged with breaking and entering a poolroom — a felony under Florida law. At his trial he asked the court to appoint a lawyer for him, but the judge refused. The U. S. Supreme Court unanimously reversed Gideon's conviction, stating: "The right of one charged with crime to counsel may not be fundamental and essential to fair trial in some countries, but it is in ours." (Later retried with competent counsel, Gideon was found not guilty.)

In the *Miranda* case, a confession was admitted as evidence

---

17. *Ibid.*, at 452-453.
18. *Mapp* v. *Ohio, supra,* 367 U.S. at 655. The Supreme Court subsequently held that this rule did not "operate retrospectively upon cases finally decided . . . prior to *Mapp.*" *Linkletter* v. *Walker,* 381 U.S. 618 (1965).

against a man charged with rape. The defendant had not been informed of his constitutional rights to remain silent and to have legal counsel. The Supreme Court reversed the conviction on grounds which a dissenting Justice expressed as follows:

> The foremost requirement, upon which later admissibility of a confession depends, is that a fourfold warning be given to a person in custody before he is questioned: namely, that he has a right to remain silent, that anything he says may be used against him, that he has a right to have present an attorney during the questioning, and that if indigent he has a right to a lawyer without charge.[19]

The case was remanded for new trial; Miranda was again found guilty, this time without the confession, and sentenced to the same term of years as in the original trial.

It is difficult to disagree with the actual decisions in these cases. Do we not want the police to be required to get a search warrant before breaking into any home? Should a poor person be tried on a felony charge without a lawyer? Do we not want the police to follow both the Constitution and the law in arrest and interrogation? We do. But if we accept these principles, we must recognize that they call, by implication, for certain improvements in law enforcement:

1. They suggest that the police should place more emphasis on investigation *before* making an arrest.
2. They may make it necessary to establish facts which point to, or demonstrate, a suspect's guilt, apart from any confession.
3. They require close attention to what really moves an officer to make an arrest or search in a given case. An action admittedly based on a mere hunch will no longer stand up in court. (Where a "hunch" actually is based on prior knowledge of a crime recently committed, and on suspicious conduct by a person under observation, it may well represent legal probable cause.)
4. They call for increased use of the judiciary to issue warrants for arrest and search.
5. They suggest compliance with state and Federal statutes requiring that a person arrested for crime must appear promptly before a judge.

---

19. *Miranda v. Arizona, supra,* 384 U.S. at 504-505 (dissenting opinion).

6. They indicate that every bar association and police department in the United States should immediately seek to devise ways and means to provide counsel for indigents.

Can anyone doubt that the requirements just outlined demand higher police training and more police manpower?

The Civil Rights Revolution

With the civil rights revolution of the 1960's, this nation has finally gone to work on the historic task of raising 11 per cent of its people from the effects of 300 years of slavery and segregation. Such an undertaking is bound to be fraught with potentially dangerous tensions. Attitudes long accepted are being openly challenged; hostilities long repressed are being overtly expressed. Obviously, the role of the police under these circumstances is both crucial and exceedingly difficult.

Three facts in particular stand out:

First, the civil rights movement has decreased Negroes' tolerance of indignities inflicted by the police, and has greatly intensified the demand for equal law enforcement. The brunt of protest and picketing on this score has been directed at the police in Northern cities. In later pages, we will deal with these problems in some detail and see what can be done about them.

Second, civil rights parades, demonstrations and meetings, no matter how peaceable in planning and execution, require considerable police manpower. Vast additional planning efforts and man hours of work invariably go into keeping legitimate protests from turning into riot.

Third, every time illegal violence is employed against civil rights demonstrations anywhere, it increases animosity against police officers everywhere. The dogs which Police Chief T. Eugene ("Bull") Connor set on young Negroes in Birmingham, Alabama, in 1963, probably caused more physical injury to police officers in other cities in the long run than to the demonstrators they were pictured as attacking. Similarly, nationwide hostility against police has been generated by failures to curb violence that was thought to have been inspired by the Ku Klux Klan, or by charges of alleged police complicity in crimes against civil rights workers.

A new difficulty, for the police as well as for the community as a whole, is that lately the direction and tone of large parts of the civil rights movement have changed.

In the 1950's and early 1960's, the civil rights emphasis was on obtaining equality for Negroes through integration with the general American community. Non-violence was the guiding idea and the sole tactic. With the active backing of many white citizens, the movement succeeded in getting legally sanctioned segregation outlawed and equal-rights laws enacted — laws forbidding discrimination in such fields as public accommodations, education, housing and employment.

But it soon became apparent that demolishing barriers would not by itself enable Negroes to make up for centuries of deprivation and demoralization. In income, employment and educational achievement, a great many Negroes actually were — and still are — falling farther behind the affluent white society. The gains just made had brought rising hopes and expectations to black Americans; but for many, the reality remained as bleak as ever.

In the past few years, the mood of many Negroes has changed from optimism to frustration, rage — and doubt that white America ever meant to fulfill its promise of equal rights. Moreover, Negroes have come to see that patient non-violence is not always the rule on the American scene — that, as Tom Wicker wrote in *The New York Times*, "except on the lips of American Negroes, or those who may speak to Negroes, the advocacy of violence has a general immunity from censure. The world puts high value on physical courage, strength and determination; in the grotesque Washington phrase, it is admirable to be 'hard-nosed.'"[20]

And so, a growing number of Negroes — disappointed in the strategy of gradualism and voluntary integration, and disillusioned with the many white allies who fell away when the going got hard — are deciding that the Negro must get tough and must "go it alone."

---

20. Tom Wicker, "The Hard-Nose Phenomenon," *The New York Times*, September 3, 1967, section 4, p. 10. Copyright 1967 by The New York Times Company. Reprinted by permission.

This sort of thinking is not entirely new. Back in the 1920's, Marcus Garvey and his followers called on "former slaves" to return to their African homeland and establish a new nation there. In the 1930's, the Communist Party gained some attention with its advocacy of "self-determination of the black belt." In the 1950's and early 1960's, while full integration was the fundamental thrust of the civil rights movement, the Black Muslims, alone and with a very limited following, kept alive the advocacy of "Negro nationalism," and gave free expression to hatred of whites. But only in recent years have Negroes in substantial numbers begun to seek alternatives to the idea of gradual integration.

The new mood, usually called "Black Power," is not yet well defined. To some Negroes, Black Power means simply a more vigorous demand by the Negro community for a fair share of the nation's wealth and opportunities. To some it means concerted efforts to strengthen Negro political influence (such as the campaigns that made possible the election of Negro mayors in Cleveland and Gary in 1967). To some — not all — it means refusal to form alliances with whites. To still others, it means a new-found, and wholesome, pride in their race and heritage.

But to some it means open, avowed hatred of white America, together with a conviction that only violence will make the nation give the Negro his due. The most alienated of this group have become determined to bring America down with them if they fail.

Riots and Violence

Mass violence in Negro-white relations is not new in this country. In this century alone, prior to 1964, there were some 50 racial clashes, mostly in the wake of the two World Wars. What is new about the outbreaks of the last few summers is that the burning, looting and sniping have usually been initiated by Negroes, not by whites as in former years.

Violence in some form as an answer to excessive frustration has occurred in just about every decade and over just about every major social issue in the nation's history. Perhaps the most remarkable thing about the Negro civil rights movement is that it refused to listen to advocates of violence, and remained a peaceful revolution, as long as it did.

The outbursts that marked the summers of 1964 and 1965 gave warning that the pace of change was too slow to allay the Negroes' 100-year frustrations. And in the spring of 1966, a new, angry mood was articulated on a freedom march in Mississippi, organized by James Meredith, the student who had earlier integrated the University of Mississippi. Meredith had labeled the demonstration a "march against fear." But among the participants was at least one who was to seize upon inspiring fear in whites as his own basic weapon: Stokely Carmichael, the leader of the left-wing Student Non-Violent Coordinating Committee.

Also present on the same march, and in obvious competition for the minds and hearts of the marchers, was the Reverend Dr. Martin Luther King, the recognized spokesman of the non-violent civil rights movement. But in this region, where three civil rights workers — James E. Chaney, Andrew Goodman and Michael Schwerner — had been murdered, and where Meredith had been shot and wounded on an earlier march, Dr. King's advocacy of Christian love seemed less appealing to many of the young and angry marchers than Carmichael's violent version of "Black Power."

Carmichael did not actually elaborate the violent connotations of his appeal on the Mississippi march. They were spelled out later by him and his associate H. Rap Brown in Dayton, Ohio, in Cambridge, Maryland, in Detroit, Michigan, and elsewhere. Their message was that American society was so controlled by racism, and so brutal in its treatment of Negro citizens that its destruction was the legitimate and proper goal of any self-respecting Negro.

It was only a logical step from this premise to the advocacy of hatred of "whitey" or "the honkies," and to a demand for complete racial separation which frequently sounds like the Ku Klux Klan's propaganda line.

While in many respects demagogues like Carmichael and H. Rap Brown have probably been products of history rather than makers of it, their individual role in shaping riot patterns cannot be ignored. In Nashville, a speech by Carmichael was followed immediately by riots. In Cambridge, Maryland, Rap Brown urged Negroes to "burn this town down," and, referring to a particular school, he said: "You should've burned it down long ago."[21] The fires which followed leveled two blocks — and the school. In Dayton, Ohio, Brown is reported to have said during the height of the Cincinnati riots: "We must help our soul brothers in Cincinnati." General as these words were, the audience in that context understood them to have an obvious meaning, and proceeded directly to riot in the streets of Dayton.

On the heels of the Detroit riot, Brown made the matter even clearer to an audience of 1,000 in the riot area by saying: "Stop looting and start shooting."[22]

A significant common feature of the Cincinnati, Newark and Detroit riots of 1967 was a pattern of hit-and-run fire bombings, which left a string of major conflagrations an eighth to a quarter of a mile apart, frequently in a straight line down major thoroughfares. There also was a pattern of selectivity in the targets: Most frequently hit were credit furniture houses, which combined high combustibility with maximum unpopularity in the ghetto areas as a result of high interest rates and hard-line repossession practices.

Firemen and police, having responded in numbers to the first half dozen of these conflagrations, rapidly found themselves drawing upon their last reserves as the fire calls continued. In Detroit, 1,322 fire alarms were registered during the four days of rioting — more than 800 over normal. Much of the time, the Fire Department had no equipment to commit to new blazes.

It seems probable that the fire bombing that turned several of the 1967 riots from spontaneous, localized disturbances into city-wide conflagrations was, at least to some degree, planned and organized. It takes some premeditation to make a Molotov cocktail. And the skip-hop pattern of fire bombing, plus the eyewitness

---

21. "Black Militants Talk of Guns and Guerrillas," *U. S. News & World Report*, August 7, 1967, p. 32.
22. "Detective Hurt in Stoning After Rap Brown Talk," *Detroit News*, August 28, 1967, section A, p. 10.

accounts of arson squads, suggest much more than just the sudden inclination of a few young people who saw an opportunity for trouble. Significantly, some of the terrorists described the civil commotions of Newark and Detroit, not in terms of riot, but in terms of insurrection, and talked openly of plans for repetition. From Cuba, Carmichael spoke of the riots as "guerrilla war."

On the other hand, the evidence must be seen in context. *Newsweek's* special edition of November 20, 1967, entitled "The Negro in America," commented:

> Obviously, black-power and Communist organizers were in the field. They may even have sparked some riots and prolonged others. But no conspiracy theory will explain four summers of rioting in more than 100 cities.[23]

White America cannot, with accuracy, blame its present great difficulties upon "outside agitators." If we have in our cities — as we do — people who are committed to guerrilla war against America, they are likely to be wholly home-grown agitators. If we ask why they should be so bitter and so alienated, they will cite 300 years of reasons, and a complacency about inequality and injustice which is still prevalent today.

When all of this is said, however, it still is true that society's concern in any premeditated violence must be very great indeed. It must be recognized for the future that two or three determined people with an automobile and some gasoline, bottles and rags can, in an hour, set ten widely spaced fires that will tie up the entire equipment of a major city's fire department. Nor should anyone assume that the tactics thus far employed represent the ultimate potential of urban guerrilla war. The utilities of a major city — water, gas, electricity and telephone — are highly vulnerable to determined attack. So are its expressways and tunnels. And there being no reason to avoid contemplation of the ultimate, so are department stores, high rise apartments, schools, hotels and hospitals. As of now, no urban police department has the manpower and capability to guard its city effectively against the ultimate potential.

---

23. "What Must Be Done," *Newsweek*, November 20, 1967, pp. 33, 35.

To date the terrorists probably have the active allegiance of far less than 1 per cent of the country's Negro population. And probably two-thirds of the Negro population has such a stake in our society as to make it reject any incitement which advocates destruction of America. Yet ordinary people do get caught up in mob violence once it starts. In some portions of the Negro population, the 1967 riots have left at least some sympathy for, and some pride in, the perpetrators of violence — even among normally staid and responsible citizens.

The other side of the picture is that violence breeds violence — that the police (and National Guard) charged with subduing rioters, looters and demagogues sometimes respond with excessive force of their own. Killings, sometimes in large numbers, have often been a feature of riot control, as in the Watts outbreak of 1965 and in those at Newark and Detroit in 1967. The Watts deaths undoubtedly had much to do with later eruptions there.

However highly trained, a policeman is not immune from fear when faced with sniping or fire bombs. But that of course does not give him the right to resort indiscriminately to fatal force instead of force appropriate to the conditions confronting him. Nor can the general impact of riot justify trigger-happy gunfire or the venting of personal race prejudice.

The police are not responsible for solving America's race problem. Doing away with urban ghettos and attaining full rights for Negroes are tasks for the nation as a whole; and viewed against the background just outlined, they take on an immediacy that should attract the most practical and hardheaded observer of the American scene.

But if we are to move toward the needed fundamental social changes without something approaching civil war, can anyone doubt the need to reexamine the role of the police in this conflict, and its capacity to meet the challenge?

THE CONFLICT BETWEEN NEGROES AND POLICE

WHAT HAS BEEN pointed to thus far shows that the current crisis in law enforcement often is most visible in the relationship between the police and the Negro community.

That relationship has rarely been happy in the past, and today it is strained to the utmost. In most American cities, policemen and poor Negroes live in what can only be described as intermittent warfare. Hostility abounds on both sides — in the minds and hearts of unemployed Negro youths on ghetto streets, and in the minds and hearts of white police officers who may have to curb ghetto violence.

Many ethnic minorities besides Negroes have experienced conflict with police in years past, and some do today: Puerto Ricans in Eastern cities, especially New York, and Spanish-speaking groups in Los Angeles and other Southwestern and Western cities. But since Negroes are the largest and most cohesive disadvantaged group in our big cities, the hostility between them and the police is the most serious of such antagonisms. If we are to devise ways of bringing the controls of civilization more effectively into play between these antagonists, we must explore the origins and the depth of the conflict.

A Legacy of Bitterness

Hostility between Negroes and police has deep roots in the past — in the long years of officially enforced and popularly sanctioned second-class citizenship for Negroes.

Until 1954, when the United States Supreme Court outlawed segregated schools and thereby sounded the death knell for all legally established segregation, the law in Southern states assigned an inferior status to all Negro citizens solely because of their color. One of the normal duties of police forces in these states was to enforce this system. Elsewhere in the country, Negroes, though technically equal to whites, were also unofficially segregated and kept in inferior status by custom and tradition. Not surprisingly, policemen in both North and South became deeply imbued with the idea that a major part of their responsibility was to "keep the Negro in his place."

Since Negroes were classed as inferior not on the basis of conduct but simply of race, police in the days before 1954 often did not need to distinguish between the law-abiding and the lawless Negro. The inevitable outcome was hostility among Negroes toward police and among police toward Negroes.

Today, the Negro citizen still tends to see the police officer with his white face as the enforcer of the white man's law, which for nearly 300 years kept his people enslaved or segregated. If he is old enough to have been a teen-ager in the 1930's, his first contact with the law, in some small Southern town, may well have been with a policeman who told him: "Nigger, don't let the sun set on you in this town!" Thirty years later, in a big Northern city, just this memory can turn a Saturday night party that has gotten loud enough for a police call into a dangerous melee.

Many people living today remember far worse things — the worst being the thousands of lynchings which were possible only because law enforcement agencies stood aside and let mobs work their will. From 1882 to 1959, 2,595 Negroes were lynched in nine Southern states.[24] No white person was ever punished for these offenses. And while lynching in the traditional form has almost disappeared from the American scene, its spirit lingers in anti-civil-rights violence, also frequently condoned by local law enforcement personnel.

In 1963, a bomb planted in a Negro church in Birmingham,

---

24. *1961 United States Commission on Civil Rights Report*, V: *Justice* (Washington, D.C.), p. 267.

Alabama, killed four small children and injured several others. The same year a Baltimore postman, William Moore, was slain near Attalla, Alabama, while on a peaceful one-man freedom march, and Medgar Evers, a well-known civil rights leader, was murdered from ambush in Jackson, Mississippi. In 1964, Chaney, Goodman and Schwerner were murdered in Philadelphia, Mississippi, and Lemuel A. Penn, a Negro army reserve colonel, was shot to death while driving through the vicinity of Colbert, Georgia. In 1965, a white Unitarian minister, the Reverend James J. Reeb, died after a beating in Selma, Alabama, and shortly afterwards, Mrs. Viola Liuzzo, a Detroit housewife, was shot to death near Hayneville, Alabama. No one responsible for any of these crimes has been convicted in a state court. It took Federal intervention to obtain convictions in the Liuzzo as well as the Chaney-Goodman-Schwerner case.

Since the school desegregation decision was handed down in 1954, the message that the United States Constitution is color-blind has slowly penetrated, at least as a principle, into most parts of the country. But attitudes, customs and conduct patterns have not yet caught up. It is no secret that the 1954 ruling and the various other prohibitions of segregation in public facilities that followed in its wake were accepted with less than alacrity by some states and local governments.

Indeed, certain governors, mayors and city councils continued to uphold unconstitutional racial restrictions, using the local police to defy Federal efforts to enforce Supreme Court rulings. In such cases, the police had to go along and try to enforce the local law — and as a result found itself ranged against the Federal power. This is what happened, for example, in the controversies over desegregating the Universities of Mississippi and Alabama, in 1962 and 1963, and in the 1965 demonstrations at Selma, Alabama.

Current Animosity

It would be comforting to think that the causes of conflict between Negroes and police all stemmed from the deep South and the past, and that present-day police practices had nothing to do with it.

Unfortunately, it would also be untrue. While the conflict between the police and the Negro people is deeply rooted in history, it is also deeply rooted in current everyday experience.

Today, the police in most of America's great cities understand that they are the public's servants, charged with keeping the law; but they do not always carry this understanding into the Negro areas. There, all too often, police tend to act like an army of occupation. Many police officers see the citizen with a black face as a potential enemy. The depth of hostility may be measured by the great number of present-day police officers who invariably use the hated term "nigger" in talking about (and sometimes to) Negro citizens. A study by the President's Crime Commission Task Force on Police found that 72 per cent of the police officers whom it interviewed in three major cities exhibited prejudice against Negroes in their responses to Task Force observers.[25]

These negative attitudes often stem only in part from traditional prejudice. Many white police officers work in poor, predominantly Negro precincts where they are constantly seeing crimes committed, but live in middle-class white neighborhoods where they have little contact with crime. As a result, they tend to identify Negroes with crime, and whites with peace and order. In addition few policemen understand why in ghetto neighborhoods hostility greets even their most routine actions — such as the arrest of a Saturday night drunk. They respond with resentment of their own.

Whatever the reason for the policeman's hostility, the people of the ghetto bitterly resent it. The millions of Negro citizens who left the South to escape the inequalities and indignities of segregation and seek a better life for themselves and their families looked upon the North as the promised land. But in this promised land they found widespread community prejudice and, together with stricter policing than back home, widespread police bias. The contrast between their hopes and the reality gives rise to frustration and anger, which are often turned against the police.

---

25. "Study Calls Police Bias Widespread," *The Washington Post*, June 29, 1967, p. A1.

Of course a great deal of the anger the policeman faces in the ghetto actually has nothing to do with him at all. For example, the police have no control over housing conditions in the ghetto. But a man who must live with his wife and ten children in two rooms is likely to be in a constant rage over these conditions; and the policeman, as the nearest representative of the world beyond the ghetto, may well bear the brunt of his fury.

Similarly, the police do not cause family discord or alcoholism. Yet a man who has just had a drunken, violent argument with his wife may, without provocation or warning, kill a policeman who seeks to give him a routine traffic ticket.

Again, the police do not create unemployment; nor are they responsible for the fact that discriminatory practices, old and new, make it much harder for Negro youngsters to find jobs than for white ones. But the Negro teen-ager, shut out of a world to which he feels he should belong, does not know the origins of his plight, and the cop on the corner becomes a symbol of the society which has turned its back on him. Given the opportunity, the teen-ager sometimes decides the cop is a good target for a rock.

Finally, both the occasional lawbreaker and the career criminal have a built-in antagonism toward the police and their work. In poor neighborhoods, the policeman has plenty of experience with both types and is constantly reminded of their hatred of what he stands for.

Negroes' Major Grievances Against Police

It is a simple fact that most Negro citizens do not believe that we have equal law enforcement in any city in this country. Whether the stated belief is well founded or not is at least partly beside the point. The existence of the belief is damaging enough.

Forms of address are a common and by no means unimportant cause of friction between police and Negro citizens. Probably 90 per cent of the police officers in the United States habitually use the term "nigger" in private conversation, and on many occasions the too familiar word slips out in the heat of an altercation. Inevitably it adds an element of passion, which can change a routine arrest into a battle, fatal to either a police officer or a civilian.

A Negro adult who is hailed by a police officer with the words, "Hey, boy," knows that this form of address would not be used for a white person. Even if the policeman is making a wholly legitimate inquiry, the tone provokes antagonism which the citizen carries away with him. The same is true when an officer making a traffic arrest addresses the offender by his first name. And the factory worker resents failure to accord him the normal title of "Mr." just as much as the more articulate middle-aged wife of a doctor resents being called "Alice" by someone she has never met.

Arrests without warrants, "for investigation," do even more to stir up hostility against police in the Negro community. Investigative arrests have never been lawful; but in most metropolitan police departments they are still accepted and hotly defended as a "necessary police tool." Two big cities, Detroit and Washington, have eliminated them as a matter of administrative policy.

The practice known as "stop and frisk" creates intense hostility. The widespread use of "stop and frisk" in the Negro, as opposed to the white, areas of big cities, confirms Negroes' suspicions about unequal law enforcement. The Negro doctor on a sick call who finds himself spread-eagled on his automobile and searched considers it (rightly!) impossible to believe that this would have happened to his white counterpart.

Experiences like these are familiar to practically all Negro citizens in Northern cities. They tend to make persons who have never experienced or seen any physical abuse by a police officer ready to believe the worst stories of police "brutality." In fact, it often turns out that vehement complaints about "brutality" actually refer to indignities like those just described.

One exceedingly sore spot in the relations between Negroes and the police has been the use of police dogs. Those who advocate the practice say, "The Negroes are scared of dogs." So is everyone else. But, as has been proved again and again, fear is the least effective and least dependable way to build a sound relationship.

To a policeman on a lonely beat, a dog may be a useful companion. Dogs also have their uses in guarding department stores and other buildings at night, when the doors are locked and no human being is supposed to be present. On the other hand, to threaten people with dogs in a tense situation having racial overtones — for example, at a civil rights demonstration — is like pouring gasoline on a fire.

Still, of all the police practices in day-to-day law enforcement that fan the flames of conflict, the most inflammatory is the actual use of excessive violence — "brutality" in the real sense — against Negroes. Under this heading come unnecessary violence at arrest, the "third degree" and what is known as "alley court," that is, deliberate roughing up of a police prisoner as punishment. "Alley court" is ordinarily used only against members of minority groups — currently the Negro population. By inflaming the feelings of that group, it deprives the police department of its most important ally in the war against crime: the overwhelming majority of residents in the core areas of the city who are law-abiding.

"Alley court" and "third degree" methods are not sanctioned by the law or the police manual, and are condemned by modern police administration. They probably are less common than the number of complaints might suggest. (In my experience, only one instance of physical abuse could be established for every five allegations of brutality.) But we cannot blink at the fact that such abuses do happen, in both Northern and Southern states. The President's Commission on Civil Rights in 1947 and the U.S. Civil Rights Commission in 1961 have documented substantial numbers of cases; and their findings leave no doubt that many of the roots of police-Negro conflict lie right there.[26]

In what we may hope is past history, brutalities of a considerably worse variety were common. There still are officers who will tell of being broken in by an older officer who walked up to an obviously drunken Negro, knocked him down with his fist, and ex-

---

26. *To Secure These Rights, op. cit.*, pp. 25-27; *The 50 States Report, op. cit.*

plained to the rookie: "That's the way we teach them respect. Now I'll pick one for you and you deck him."

Not infrequently in the past, there also were outright police executions — usually of persons captured after killing a policeman. The "executioners" in such cases were usually exonerated by each other's testimony, and by the understandable outrage which prosecutors, judges and juries felt over the murder of a policeman. In this way, revenge would prevail over police discipline, whose final test is the capture, alive and intact, of the individual charged with a crime.

Less often recognized as a source of friction is the use of fatal force that may be technically within the law. In these instances the police may shoot a fleeing person whom they have reason to believe to be a felon.[27] But often that person can be stopped or apprehended by other means; and even more often he may pose no threat to anyone's life. In a disproportionate number of cases, the victims are Negroes. Such killings frequently inflame public opinion and on occasion have triggered riots.

Hardly less important than the Negroes' complaints about what the police do wrong are their complaints about what the police fail to do. Perhaps the sorest point is insufficient policing.

There is a tendency in assigning police patrols to take area and population primarily into account, with too little attention paid to the amount of crime. Other frequent complaints have to do with police response in emergencies, which is often less rapid in the ghetto than elsewhere, and with police investigation (and prosecution) of crimes, which is thought to be less effective there.

Finally, Negroes are rightly incensed over failure to stamp out organized crime. Most middle-class citizens in most cities are unaware of the extent of "syndicate" operations, because racketeers rarely maintain publicly known locations in the better neighborhoods. But in poor areas, especially in Negro ghettos, organized

---

27. The common law prohibits use of fatal force for the apprehension of anyone for an offense less than a felony.

crime frequently operates on such a scale that it is widely known. And if the people of a given neighborhood see that racketeering is tolerated, they assume that the police are in league with the operators. They know that wherever a numbers house, a walk-in bookie, an unlicensed drinking place or a house of prostitution operates openly, there must be corruption, whether in the local precinct or higher up, at Headquarters or City Hall.

Why Negroes Need Police Most

Negroes, then, resent the policeman, but they need him, and they know it. In New York's Harlem and Los Angeles' Watts, a year after these areas were torn by riots, public-opinion surveys found both widespread hostility against police and widespread desire for more and better police protection.

To the slum dweller, there is no contradiction in these two responses. For no portion of our society has a greater stake in effective, vigilant, vigorous law enforcement than do Negroes in the big cities. All the statistics underscore that Negroes are more likely to be victims of crime — particularly crimes of violence — than are whites.

Thus, in Washington, a few years ago, 84 per cent of assault victims were Negroes, according to an article in *Look* magazine (June 4, 1963). In a largely Negro precinct in Detroit, a study observed that 78 per cent of identified assault offenders were Negroes, but 76 per cent of assault victims also were Negroes. Similarly, a study of homicides in Dallas, conducted in 1963, found 68 per cent of suspects in homicides were Negroes, but so were 69 per cent of the victims.

As for crimes involving both whites and Negroes, a nationwide report dated 1964 indicates that such cases are relatively rare:

> National and official crime statistics do not provide data, but enough research has been conducted to permit the definite statement that criminal homicide, like most other assaultive offenses, is predominantly an intra-group, intraracial act. In a detailed five-year study of homicides in Philadelphia (1948-1952), it was noted that in 516, or 94 per cent, of the 550 identified relationships, the victim and offender were members of the

same race. Hence, in only 34, or 6 percent, of these homicides did an offender cross the race line: 14 were Negro victims slain by whites, and 20 were whites slain by Negroes.[28]

In any event, whatever the relative incidence of crimes committed by Negroes, overwhelming percentages of the Negro population in any big American city are basically law-abiding in terms of both felony records and attitudes. In some cities, these percentages run as high as 90 per cent. The question is how to turn the 90 per cent into active supporters of law and order. For no police force can function effectively unless it has the cooperation and confidence of a large majority of the public.

---

28. Marvin E. Wolfgang, *Crime and Race: Conceptions and Misconceptions* (New York: Institute of Human Relations Press, 1964), p. 38.

19th-CENTURY TOOLS FOR 20th-CENTURY TASKS

PROBABLY the chief reason for the shortcomings of police work today — in the area of race relations and elsewhere — is that society has not materially changed in its attitudes toward the police in a hundred years. Despite the vast expansion of police functions, there has been little updating in the staffing and organization of police forces, in the qualifications expected of the police officer, or in his status, weapons or pay. The police forces of this country are essentially 19th-century organizations on which society has loaded 20th-century problems.

Outdated Standards and Lagging Status

As in the last century, we still recruit relatively poorly educated, poorly trained men for police work. We pay them about what we pay unskilled factory workers — something like $5,000 a year on the national average. We think of the policeman's job as basically physical. His strongest weapon, we feel, is his fist. And for added help we give him the same weapons we gave his grandfather. Arnold Sagalyn, formerly Director of Law Enforcement Coordination for the United States Treasury, has characterized the policeman's weaponry as follows:

> [A] police officer today must still depend on the same weapons which were standard equipment for our police nearly 100 years ago—the police stick and a lethal gun.... The limitations and ineffectiveness of the police officer's weapons leave him dangerously exposed to the hazards he faces in his work.[29]

The social status of police is also a carry-over from the 19th

---

29. Arnold Sagalyn, Remarks before the National Symposium on Law Enforcement Science and Technology — Session on Weaponry, Chicago, March 9, 1967, p. 1.

century. The policeman still ranks so low on the value scale of present-day public opinion that thousands of young men pass up challenging and fascinating police jobs for employment in factories, the post office or welfare departments.

The educational requirements for policemen, in most cities, are as low as their pay. In particular, the training that policemen receive in the social aspects of their job is still in its infancy. Few are systematically helped to understand the causes of the abnormal conditions — poverty, unemployment, delinquency, drug addiction, apathy — which they encounter on the job every day. And few are being taught to understand how the world looks from the point of view of persons affected by these problems.

Meanwhile, most police officers live in relative isolation from the rest of society. They not only work with other police officers; they also tend to bowl with them, drink with them, hunt with them, go to church with them. Their wives, too, socialize mostly with one another.

Since relatively few policemen are Negroes or members of other disadvantaged minority groups, the overwhelming majority of police officers have no social relationships with Negroes. Few have ever spent a social evening with a Negro or received one into their homes. This state of affairs does not help the groups understand, or deal with, one another on a basis of equality. Thus, the conflict between Negroes and the police actually is a conflict between two of the most segregated groups in American society.

Obsolete Organization

In addition to all these handicaps, the opproximately 400,000 police officers responsible for day-by-day law enforcement in the United States are split up into some 40,000 separate and largely autonomous jurisdictions — Federal, state, county and local.

The nearest thing we have to a national police service is the Federal Bureau of Investigation. This relatively small, highly professional body has general jurisdiction over all violations of Federal laws which are not within the specific province of any other specialized Federal agency. But it has no jurisdiction over local law enforcement.

Each of the 50 states has a central police organization, usually called the State Police, whose work consists mostly of patrolling state highways. These forces generally do not get involved in local law enforcement unless a local sheriff or police chief asks for aid.

Below the state level, the more than 3,000 county governments maintain their own police. In most of them, a sheriff is the principal law enforcement officer. Usually he is an elected official, whose powers in the areas of law enforcement and carrying out court orders are spelled out by state law. Most often, he and his force operate chiefly in unincorporated areas, and work in municipalities only in conjunction with city police. In many places, however, unincorporated townships have police departments of their own, which operate in much the same fashion as city departments.

Yet, when all is said and done, the police function in the United States is primarily a local function, governed at the municipal level. There are 17,000 separate municipal police units in the country, ranging from one-man village forces to New York City's 28,000-man department. No national law or practice sets standards for all these units. Whatever degree of uniformity exists in standards of hiring, pay or conduct is chiefly due to custom or mutual communication — and to the work of the International Association of Chiefs of Police, a professional organization, which increasingly provides for exchange of information, ideas and methods.

Besides raising problems of efficiency, local control can make the police a pawn in struggles between City Hall or the state house and Washington — as has happened in the confrontations over Negro rights in the South noted earlier.

Decentralized, local control of police also accounts, in large measure, for the objectionable police and court practices that have figured so large in the civil rights debates of the 1960's — among them: investigative arrests, detention without prompt judicial hearing, improper methods of police interrogation, and denial of the citizen's right to refuse to testify against himself, or to confront and cross-examine his accuser. As we have seen, these topics have been progressively clarified by constitutional decisions of the United States Supreme Court and by lower Federal and state courts. But it is a long way from the Supreme Court, and its increasing concern for securing constitutional liberties, to the police officer on the city street, whose main concern is order. That is one big reason why national civil rights policy has been so slow in being translated into practice.

The Role of the Community

Institutions do not exist in a vacuum; they are shaped by the values and attitudes of the society in which they have their being. Thus, a police force in a democratic society can only be as good as the people want it to be; and to bring American law enforcement into the 20th century is a job for the community as well as for police administrators, or the public officials from whom the administrators take their orders.

The fact of the matter is that most citizens show little concern for the day-to-day work and the professional needs of police. Having delegated the task of guarding their safety to the policeman, they promptly forget about it — and him. But the policeman cannot function at his best as a forgotten man. Efficient law enforcement and, equally important, fair law enforcement, must always be a joint enterprise of the police and the public.

This does not mean that private individuals may go out and play policeman in the manner of vigilantes. It does mean that citizens, black and white, must demand first-rate policing and supply both the means and the cooperation which it requires.

Efforts and influence on behalf of better law enforcement can be brought to bear at every level: on the block, at the station house, at City Hall, at the State House and in Washington. Citizens can make themselves heard as individuals or, more effectively, through their organizations — for example, through block clubs, neighborhood associations, civil rights groups, churches, service clubs, labor unions, chambers of commerce, social service organizations, human relations agencies, and even through special associations created for the purpose. A later chapter will outline some of the ways in which citizens can work toward higher standards of law enforcement in their communities.

RECOMMENDATIONS IN BRIEF

The situation in American cities suggests three general objectives for any 20th-century police force:
1. More law enforcement and more effective law enforcement.
2. Equal protection of the law for all law-abiding citizens; equal enforcement of the law against all law violators.
3. The support of all law-abiding citizens for enforcement.

Official adoption and publication of these objectives by police departments may prove to be significant and helpful both to the police officers inside the department and to citizens outside.

However, generalities like these rapidly become meaningless if they are not translated into specifics. How to do that is the subject of the chapters that follow. They suggest steps by which any police command can move from the general principles to concrete action in its critical relationships with racial minorities, beginning with the issues identified earlier as the Negro community's main grievances. They also point out specific ways in which citizens can help obtain adequate, properly run police protection for everyone.

A chapter-by-chapter summary of the most essential recommendations follows:

POLICE PROFESSIONALIZATION:

Forbid use of racial slurs and other "trigger words" by policemen.

Replace rudeness with good manners, starting with the giving of traffic tickets.

End investigative arrests.

Ban the use of police dogs in core areas of cities.

End "alley court" (police punishment).

Identify troublemakers on the police force and transfer them to non-critical jobs.

THE DISCIPLINED USE OF FORCE:

Set clear standards for the proper use of force.

Promote the development of more effective, less destructive weapons.

Press for national and state regulation (including registration) of firearms.

Train police to deal properly with disturbed persons.

MORE — AND MORE EFFECTIVE — LAW ENFORCEMENT:

Increase law enforcement in high-crime precincts.

Devise methods for faster police response.

Drive out organized crime, paying particular attention to core areas.

EFFECTIVE RACE RIOT CONTROL:

Maintain steady communications between Negroes and police to insure citizen cooperation in times of trouble.

Provide for rapid mobilization and deployment of anti-riot forces.

Meet racial disturbances with well-trained, disciplined, integrated forces in adequate numbers.

Keep curiosity seekers and known inciters of riots out of trouble areas.

Set up stand-by arrangements with state and national military forces.

CHANNELS OF COMMUNICATION:

Organize for day-to-day contact with all sections of the community.

Deal courteously and cooperatively with potentially hostile organizations.

Provide for direct staff investigation of complaints from the public, and for final decisions on such complaints by the highest civilian authority in the police department.

ORGANIZING CITIZEN SUPPORT:

Police initiatives

Actively seek the cooperation of all citizens for law enforcement, particularly in high-crime areas.

Make it understood that improved crime control will produce an increase in the number of crimes reported, independent of actual incidence.

Community initiatives

Step up community involvement with law enforcement.

Help police obtain needed financing, manpower, equipment.

Support programs to overcome young people's hostility against police, and to interest them in police careers.

Help dispel distorted images of police in the community.

Seek business backing for programs to counter community tensions.

TOWARD A 20TH-CENTURY POLICE FORCE:

Integrate police forces; actively seek to attract members of minority groups to police careers, and help them qualify.

Improve the professional standards, training facilities and pay scales of police; enlarge forces to lower case loads.

Seek Federal assistance, particularly for college-level police training.

POLICE PROFESSIONALIZATION

MOST POLICE officers and all police administrators in America subscribe to the concept that the American policeman is a servant of the public. They see the police officer of the future as a professional, whose competence and performance warrant both self-respect and the public's support.

Unfortunately, some police officers are habitually rude and disrespectful in their dealings with some of the public. And some — few in terms of percentages, but many in absolute numbers — are sincerely convinced that peace and order cannot be maintained in American cities unless they take it upon themselves to administer physical punishment to those they think deserve it. This idea, of course, is contrary to our basic law and has no sanction in public opinion. What is more, it inevitably sets large segments of the public against the police.

"Trigger Words" and Rudeness

The use of derogatory group names like "nigger," "wop," or "kike" is so widespread among Americans that it may take a generation to eradicate them from common speech. So is habitual failure to accord minority group members the normal courtesy titles of "Mr.," "Mrs." or "Miss." But as far as police work is concerned, "trigger words," disrespectful forms of address and other discourtesies can be banned right now. Without criticizing the vocabulary used in a gunfight, police administrators can see to it that their men do not respond to mere provocative language with similar language, and can impose appropriate reprimands or penalties when this rule is violated.

To be effective, this policy must start at the top. If a patrolman knows that his inspector (or police chief) habitually uses hate words in private conversation, he will not believe that the order forbidding him to do so carries much conviction behind it.

An example of the command needed was issued in 1966 by Acting Police Commissioner George M. Gelston of Baltimore:

> It is directed that all citizens will be addressed by the appropriate title of "Mr.," "Mrs." or Miss," and that no epithets such as "wop," "kike," "polack," "nigger," etc., or "boy," "girl," etc., when addressed to adults, will be used.
>
> The dignity and professional status of this department is on the line; we either prove that this is a professional police department or not by our actions with the public.
>
> Regardless of the situation there is no excuse for an officer to become irritated or lose his temper while on duty.
>
> Any member of the department who feels he cannot abide by the above should submit his resignation.
>
> Any violation of the above will result in disciplinary action, to include discharge.
>
> I have complete confidence that all members will cooperate and enhance the position of this department in the eyes of the public by courtesy and understanding action at all times.[30]

A promising place to start changing bad police manners into good is in the giving of traffic tickets. Citizens will notice the improvement at once, because traffic control accounts for the greatest number of contacts between them and the police. The effect on Negro citizens is particularly important, for when Negroes see that the tone of traffic policing has improved, it can substantially influence their attitudes toward the police in general.

Politeness in traffic control is easy to enforce, because every police department receives many complaints about discourteous traffic policemen in the mail. (Evidently, people who drive automobiles improperly are more articulate, on the average, than those

---

30. Richard Severo, "Strong Police Command Vital to Avert More City Violence," *The Washington Post*, June 30, 1966, section A, p. 6.

arrested for other violations.) A number of police departments have instituted very successful programs to promote politeness in traffic arrests.

Investigative Arrests; "Stop and Frisk"

The Fourth Amendment to the United States Constitution prohibits arrest without "probable cause." Yet, as noted earlier, "stop and frisk" street searches and investigative arrests are common police practices in the Negro neighborhoods of many cities.

In the interest of both practicality and legality, police departments should accept the restriction that they cannot arrest a person without reason to believe that he has committed a crime. If they do have such reason, they have not only the right but the duty to arrest. Of course, police can approach any citizen they are curious about and ask him any questions they want — so long as they leave him free to refuse to answer, and do not keep him from departing when they cannot lawfully arrest him. The fact is that the vast majority of citizens approached thus by police respond vocally to any question and make no effort to terminate the conversation. Of course, if the conversation turns from general questioning into interrogation of a suspect, the warnings provided by *Miranda* v. *Arizona*, 384 U.S. 436 (1966) may be required.

Police departments should insist that suspects be booked for specific crimes, or not at all. If a man has been caught at 2 a.m. stepping out of a broken store window with his arms full of groceries, he should not be booked for "investigation of breaking and entering." He should be booked for "breaking and entering."

In many cities, however, police officers still book a suspect arrested for a specific crime as having been arrested for "investigation" of that crime. What they really mean is: "We have not yet done everything we want done about this investigation before we go to court." Of course, that is not the issue at all. The question is whether the police have a valid reason — "probable cause" — for believing that a crime has been committed and that the person arrested is the culprit.

Investigative arrests should be eliminated, as a matter of law and of administrative policy, in every jurisdiction in the country. True, this will not necessarily end improperly made arrests for which a specific offense is recorded. But experience suggests that these, too, will be fewer when a ban on investigative arrests demands more thorough advance police work.

It is most unfortunate that the Advisory Committee of the American Law Institute, in a proposed draft of a Model Code of Pre-Arraignment Practices, has lent its weight to the form of investigative arrest called "stop and frisk." The Code would authorize 20 minutes of forcible street detention with search where "the officer suspects but does not have reasonable cause to believe that a felony or misdemeanor has been committed."

The statutory standards proposed for such detention are so vague as to be of doubtful constitutionality. In a crucial case, the United States Supreme Court held arrests for search or investigation to be contrary to the Fourth Amendment. The Court said:

> When the officers interrupted the two men and restricted their liberty of movement, the arrest, for purposes of this case, was complete.... [A]n arrest is not justified by what the subsequent search discloses. *Under our system suspicion is not enough for an officer to lay hands on a citizen.*[31]

And in a more recent case the United States Supreme Court held, in effect, that where a person has been "deprived of his freedom of action in any significant way" he has been "seized" as far as the Fourth Amendment is concerned.[32]

There is no way, in my judgment, to reconcile this language with the proposed Model Code's "stop and frisk" section.

Police Dogs

The use of police dogs in core areas of cities is wrong on practical and moral counts. It is also far more dangerous than is usually acknowledged by its defenders.

---

31. *Henry* v. *U.S.*, 361 U.S. 98, 103-104 (1959). (Emphasis added.) Further doubt is cast on "stop and frisk" by *Shuttlesworth* v. *Birmingham*, 382 U.S. 87 (1966), and *Thompson* v. *City of Louisville*, 362 U.S. 199 (1960).
32. *Miranda* v. *Arizona*, 384 U.S. 436, 444 (1966).

In cold fact, police dogs are highly unreliable. At a recent police meeting, dog handlers showed how they could make a dog grab a man and then let go on command. But that night, a group of police administrators went on the street with a dog crew, and the operator of the crew said: "You saw that demonstration? The dog they showed you is the only one we have that will let go on command. I have arrested 17 people with my dog here, and she has chewed up 16 of them."

Extensive experiments were made with police dogs in the 1950's, to discover whether dogs could be successfully used as a crime-fighting tool. The findings: First, dogs could not be accurately directed at a particular individual, but often mauled innocent citizens. This naturally produced a hostile public reaction. Second, the police dog operators and their families became captives of the dogs; no one else could approach them, feed them or care for them without real hazard. The experiments were soon abandoned.

The fundamental question about police dogs is this: If it is so difficult (and it often is) for police officers and judges to tell who is guilty, how can you expect a dog to do so?

"Alley Court"

Cases of "alley court" often are not reported by the victims, and even when they are, the victim may be afraid to testify, or may make an extremely poor witness. For these reasons such episodes are rarely subject to correction by trial boards or courts.

Nonetheless, any alert, determined police administration will know when such things occur, and can put an end to them — by vigorously investigating each lead, by emphatically refusing to tolerate brutality, and by enforcing this refusal through its assignment, promotion and demotion powers.

"Alley court" episodes may stem from a police officer's basic attitude, his frustrations, or both. Policemen with reputations for courage and aggressiveness in law enforcement are rarely involved in such occurrences. More often the guilty party will be a desk officer, or a policeman who is a notorious laggard in action.

The officer who finds it necessary to demonstrate his superiority by physical violence usually picks a weak or defenseless victim: a drunk, a homosexual, a juvenile delinquent, a manacled prisoner brought to the precinct station by others. In a typical case, a policeman came across a teen-age crap game in an alley and caught three of the youngsters. He undoubtedly realized that an arrest was futile because he could not be sure who had been handling the dice or the money. His reaction on receiving denials was to beat up the boys and let them go.

The relatively few police officers who believe in "alley court" cannot be allowed to perpetuate an utterly indefensible institution. After all, the police officer is neither prosecutor, judge nor jury; his job is to identify violators of the law, to arrest them, and to bring them as peacefully and intact as possible before the judicial authority that will determine guilt and punishment. In the words of a recent policy statement by the International Association of Chiefs of Police, "the police are not in the punishing business any more than they are in the rehabilitating business. The police job is to prevent crime and to detect and apprehend offenders. Treatment of the offender is someone else's job."[33]

Troublemakers on the Force

A disproportionate amount of trouble in ghetto areas is caused by police officers who have short-fused tempers or sadistic impulses, or who simply lack common sense in crisis situations. They should be assigned to non-critical jobs. At one time, it was hoped that men with such defects could be identified through psychiatric tests at induction or later. Unfortunately, to date, this hope has not been borne out by experience. But after some years on the force, a police officer's record usually will show whether or not he ought to be in a scout car in a difficult precinct.

A policeman known to be strongly prejudiced against Negroes should not be working in a central-city Negro area; he should be transferred to an outlying precinct inhabited by whites, and may

---

33. *The Police and the Civil Rights Act* (International Association of Chiefs of Police, 1964), p. 15.

prove satisfactory there. In the same way, an officer whose record shows that a suspicious number of people have been injured in the course of his arrests should be taken off the firing line.

Of course, care must be taken that this policy does not remove from critical work those men who are simply more brave and aggressive than most. But the distinction between the brave and the brutal is not hard to draw. The valiant officer demonstrates his courage in dealing with armed robbers, in fires or other real dangers; he does not ordinarily bring in a Saturday night drunk battered with a night stick.

Police departments have a good many jobs to which policemen who lack the coolness and judgment of a good patrol officer can be assigned. The precinct commanders, who know the potential troublemakers, should be required to review their personnel periodically with such assignment criteria in mind.

THE DISCIPLINED USE OF FORCE

It is one of the contradictions of civilization that the maintenance of peace, which is the basic mission of the police, should so frequently demand the employment of force. But no one who has had contact with unreasoning drunks, armed psychotics or armed bandits — or with rioters, looters and snipers — can doubt that on occasion the police must use force to protect "domestic tranquility."

It is often overlooked that the police mission at such times is different from a military operation. The military normally seeks to strike with sufficient force to destroy the enemy. The police are supposed to employ only the minimum force necessary to gain obedience to law. In fact, it is the duty of the police, wherever possible, to protect the offender even while subduing him. And this task must be performed within all the limitations of the law.

Force and Its Aftermath

In Nashville, Tennessee, on a day in March 1967, Ramsey W. Hall, 26, a top-notch graduate student at Vanderbilt University, and normally a gentle and restrained man, began to act strangely. From a phone in a grocery store, he proposed to a girl he hardly knew, talking incoherently, crying and laughing. A policeman was called and drove him home.

That night, Hall spoke wildly to his landlady, kicking the door to her apartment. She called police and asked the three officers who arrived just to talk to him, but Hall rebuffed them. Suddenly he went berserk, pushed the landlady down a flight of stairs and started swinging at the officers, all of whom were smaller than he.

Patrolman Joseph W. Jackson hit him on the head with his night stick. The stick broke; Hall grabbed it and hit Jackson, who then drew his pistol and fired six times, killing Hall.

The police administration and the public prosecutor quickly termed the killing "justifiable homicide." Nevertheless, Nashville citizens were up in arms. Further state and Federal investigations have probed more deeply but, to date, inconclusively. Two questions remain unanswered: Civilians may reasonably ask why three armed policemen could not subdue a berserk young man without killing him; and policemen may ask how many times an officer has to be hit over the head with a club before he is justified in using his ultimate weapon.

In the Hall case, both the offender and the policemen were white. Far greater conflict is likely when a Negro is killed, even justifiably, by white police.

On a July night in 1962, in Detroit, a speeding automobile passed two police officers in a scout car. During the chase that followed, the officers were able to read the license number and to identify it from the day's "hot car" list as having been recently stolen. After a hazardous pursuit, the stolen car crashed over a curb into a bridge abutment. The driver jumped out and fled on foot. The two officers called on him to halt, and then one opened fire with his service revolver. One shot went home, at about 50 yards distance, and the driver fell dead, with a bullet in his head. He was six feet tall, weighed 140 pounds, was 14 years old and had recently escaped from the Wayne County Training School. He also was a Negro. The officers were white.

If, as seems likely, the officers had no way of knowing that the driver of the stolen car was a juvenile, their actions were within their discretion, and within the letter of Michigan law and the police manual. Just the same, a mentally disturbed 14-year-old boy was dead; and the public protest against the killing for a time seriously endangered a program, just launched, for improving relations between the Negro community and the police.

Confrontations of this sort can actually produce full-scale riots, as in the following instance, reported in October 1966:

It had a familiar, tragic ring. Alvin Johnson, a 51-year-old San Francisco policeman, spotted two Negro boys running from a car (later reported stolen) in the Hunters Point Negro ghetto last Tuesday. He shouted at them to stop, fired warning shots and then fired at them. Matthew Johnson, 16, slumped to the ground, dead.

And then Hunters Point—and later the nearby predominantly Negro Fillmore district—exploded. Mobs, composed mainly of teen-agers, rampaged through the streets, hurling rocks, burning, looting. When the police were unable to quell the rioting, the National Guard was called out. After three days, with more than 300 people under arrest and scores more injured, a tenuous calm had returned.[34]

When Is Force Proper?

The decision to employ force is the most critical of all decisions police must make. Of necessity, the policeman on the scene of an emergency has broad discretion vested in him by law — broader than that accorded to any other public official. For example, in the case of a fleeing felon, the officer's discretion may range all the way from doing nothing to killing. Where an officer's life is in danger, the law requires that those who may later review his actions place themselves in the exact situation he faced.

It would be a great service to law enforcement if the conditions that justify policemen in using their ultimate weapons were more accurately spelled out. Wherever the law can effectively and safely predetermine police reactions involving force, it should do so. Police Commissioner Howard R. Leary of New York recently limited the use of lethal weapons to three circumstances:

> If the crime was a felony involving the use or threatened use of deadly force.
>
> If the suspect is trying to escape by using a deadly weapon.
>
> If the suspect otherwise indicates that unless apprehended immediately he is likely to endanger human life or inflict serious physical injury.[35]

In his order, Commissioner Leary raised the moral question

---

34. "After Progress and Riots," *The New York Times*, October 2, 1966, section 4, p. 1. Copyright 1966 by The New York Times Company. Reprinted by permission.

35. "Leary to Impose Police Gun Curbs," *The New York Times*, March 22, 1967, pp. 1, 58.

whether it was "proper to take the life of a fleeing felon who, if caught, tried and convicted, could not be executed." He pointed out that the traditional rule under which any fleeing felon could be shot at unless he could be easily captured was "left behind from the day when all felonies were capital crimes," and stressed that felonies include "many minor crimes which do not involve the slightest risk to human life or limb." Ordinary car theft is a case in point. The thief is likely to be a juvenile, and his killing by police, even if lawful, is hard to defend on moral grounds. It is not surprising that such deaths create problems between the police and the community that may outweigh their deterrent value.

Nelson A. Watson, Project Supervisor in the Research and Development Section of the International Association of Chiefs of Police, recently suggested these standards:

No action taken by an officer in defending himself, up to and including the death of his assailant, is brutal provided:

— He is acting officially as a policeman within the boundaries of his legal powers.
— He has sufficient cause, as would appear real and reasonable to a prudent man, to fear for his personal safety.
— The means and the force employed by him are not such as a prudent man would consider excessive, unreasonable, or unnecessary.
— There is no acceptable alternative available to him considering his obligation not to retreat from his official mission and his inherent right to protect himself.

When it comes to bringing a specific police mission to a successful conclusion—getting the job done—and there is no immediate or apparent danger calling for self-defense by the officer, his actions should be tempered by good judgment, common sense, restraint, and understanding. His actions would not fall within the definition of brutality provided:

— He is acting officially as a policeman within the restrictions imposed on him by law.
— He conducts himself impartially and dispassionately.
— He is firm without being angrily unreasonable.
— He provides reasonable opportunity for compliance with the law.
— He uses force only after other means have failed.
— The force employed is not more than is required to produce compliance.
— The force is not of an uncivilized or cruel nature.

This proposed framework rules out any application of force after a person has submitted to arrest or complied with legal police orders.[36]

Better Weaponry

Plainly, society's interest would be better served if the principals in occurrences like those just described could be taken into custody without hazard to police officers or injury to themselves. Whether it can be done depends in part on our success in providing police with weapons appropriate to their present-day tasks. Here is a comment on that topic by Arnold Sagalyn, some of whose observations were cited in an earlier chapter:

> Our obsolescent, 19th century police weapons are jeopardizing the safety of more than just our police. They are also posing a danger to the peace and welfare of our urban communities. In the past few years there has been increasing evidence that the employment of these same defensive weapons—particularly the gun—to enforce the law and maintain civil order is creating far worse problems than those the police are attempting to solve.
>
> For the police officer's basic weapon, his gun, lacks the flexible response capability needed to deal with the specific type of problem involved. The inability of the police officer to control the degree and deadliness of this physical force in proportion to the nature and quality of the threat has put him—indeed the entire community—in a critical dilemma.[37]

To date, no easy answers have been forthcoming. It has been suggested that anesthesia could be administered by dart gun (as is done so effectively on TV!); but the time lost until the compound takes effect could be fatal to an officer. Besides, at the present stage of knowledge, the dosage would have to be adjusted to the size of the person to be anesthetized, lest it kill him — a complication few emergencies would permit.

To provide the police with workable new options in handling arrests is a task to which more of America's scientific knowledge should be devoted. Some new possibilities already exist — for example, a liquid, non-lethal gas, which adheres to the clothing of an offender and serves to immobilize him, and projectiles of

---

36. *The Police and the Civil Rights Act, op. cit.*, pp. 13-14.
37. Sagalyn, *op. cit.*, pp. 2-3.

brightly colored dye that can be used to mark rioters or fleeing crime suspects for later arrest. Meanwhile, some time-tested weapons deserve to be used more. For example, tear gas and bayonets are better for clearing a street than rifle or machinegun fire.

Firearms Control

England for generations has sent its policemen to their jobs without guns, and still does, notwithstanding an increase in violence during recent years. In this country, there is no point in discussing the disarming of police until we become mature enough to end the outrageously easy distribution of guns, which supplies our criminal population with its arsenals — and which made possible the assassination of President John F. Kennedy.

Lethal weapons are not subject to any kind of registration in most states. They are freely sold by mail order, with no questions asked. To reduce the chances of fatal encounters between one citizen and another, or between citizens and police, the following legislative steps are urgently needed:

1. National and state regulation of the sale of all firearms. National and state legislation prohibiting the sale of concealed weapons to, and the possession of such weapons by, civilians without permit. National and state legislation requiring registration of rifles and shotguns.
2. State legislation making illegal any resistance to arrest, even to an arrest that is later found unlawful. A decision to this effect was recently handed down by the New Jersey Supreme Court.[38]
3. Specific legal definition of the circumstances under which fatal force may be used against an unarmed felon seeking to escape. Such force might well be prohibited in cases of ordinary car theft.

Dealing With Disturbed Persons

Violence is particularly likely to arise in dealing with disturbed people, some of whom may be potentially dangerous. The policeman must learn to deal properly with such persons. He cannot, of course, be expected to practice psychiatry on the street; yet the better he understands that disorderly persons are often persons

---

38. *State* v. *Koonce*, 89 N.J. Super 169, 214A.2d 428 (1965).

whose lives are in disorder, the better able he will be to handle the problems they pose. By the way he talks to a drunk, a mental case, or a husband and wife in a fight, he can often make force unnecessary, and in some cases may even save his own life.

A police officer will be most successful in dealing with psychotics, drunks or marital battlers if he knows the importance of his job, has fundamental self-respect, and from that self-respect derives a concern for others. Humor will help him if it is the right variety — not the kind that makes jokes at the expense of others or enjoys their embarrassment, but the kind that helps him and others to tolerate peculiar situations, and even to enjoy some of them. As Dr. John M. Dorsey of Wayne State University has said:

> The policeman, or policewoman, is a most important government official. And nothing can develop his own self-respect more than his seeing and recognizing the true greatness of his career as guardian of the peace of our society. Once a police officer, on his own, succeeds in seeing ... his real position of honor in his American Government, he increases his most useful power, namely, good natured self-confidence. Good humor can keep him out of more trouble than he can ever guess without it; quite as ill humor can get him into more trouble than he can ever guess without it.[39]

It helps, too, if a police officer can show that he understands the problem or condition of the other person. A drunk who would disregard a direct, abrupt order, might cooperate when told good-naturedly: "Sure, I know how it is on a Saturday night, but we have got to get you home." And it helps even more if the officer can get it across that he is reasonable and expects the other person to be reasonable too.

---

39. John M. Dorsey, *Authority and the Police Officer* (unpublished speech, 1967).

MORE—AND MORE EFFECTIVE— LAW ENFORCEMENT

No SOUND program for improving police-community relations can be launched without strengthening law enforcement. That means more police and more effective methods for police. It also means more emphasis upon the integrity of our police forces, for no such program can succeed until citizens are convinced of the police's integrity — something they only too often have reason to doubt.

More Police Protection Where Needed

Assignments of police patrols ought not to be based simply on the size and population of an area. While, of course, no area of the city can be left without an effective patrol, the incidence of crime should be reckoned with as a vital factor in the deployment of forces. Accurate accumulation of crime statistics (as well as automobile accident statistics) and rapid calculations made from them by computers can now aid police departments to shift their manpower in accordance with actual work loads.

If law enforcement is to be equal, and if the decaying centers of cities are to be adequately policed, articulate citizens must put their influence behind efforts to secure more police. According to the National Crime Commission, local police forces as now operated cost, on a national average, $11.25 per capita per year.[40] The overwhelming majority of taxpayers probably would agree that this item of municipal expenditure should be increased.

---

40. *Task Force Report: The Police*, President's Commission on Law Enforcement and Administration of Justice (Washington, 1967), p. 7.

Faster Responses

A basic part of any program to equalize law enforcement must be to make police responses to emergency calls as prompt in central ghettos as they are in outlying residential areas. By the same token, crimes should be investigated and prosecuted as promptly in the ghetto as elsewhere. The reason is strikingly illustrated in Claude Brown's book about his youth in Harlem, *Manchild in the Promised Land*.[41] The turning point in the narrator's life comes when the police arrest the man who has just robbed and stabbed his mother. The arrest relieves him of the necessity to kill the robber, as his code would otherwise have required.

Faster mobilization of police emergency forces makes for more effective and less bloody law enforcement. It is axiomatic that the greater the police presence at a given disturbance, the less likelihood that force will have to be used. A drunk confronted by a single policeman may well try to resist arrest; but if that policeman could summon others to his aid within minutes, the chances are that the drunk would go quietly. Similarly, four police officers beleaguered by an angry crowd of 100 might well have to shoot to save their own lives, whereas 20 officers on the same scene probably could handle any problem short of gunfire from the crowd without fatal force.

Better means of rapid mobilization are available than most metropolitan police forces now use. No foot patrolman in the United States should be without a walkie-talkie radio; and every major police department should have a communication system as efficient as the one recently installed in Chicago. For even a few seconds saved in dispatching mobile units to a scene of violence can make all the difference.

Driving Out Organized Crime

Failure to stamp out organized crime — particularly in ghetto areas, where rackets tend to operate blatantly — goes far toward defeating plans for improved law enforcement and police-community relations by convincing the community that the police are

---

41. Claude Brown, *Manchild in the Promised Land* (New York: Macmillan, 1965), pp. 402-405.

corrupt. It also hampers law enforcement by publicizing the success of wrongdoing. Teen-age youngsters in the slums know the numbers man with the $200 silk suits and the shiny Cadillac as the fellow who has "made it." They want to be like him, and they quickly take on his contempt for the law, his conviction that all police officers can be bribed and that anything can be "fixed."

Organized crime forms a vast empire in these United States. No big city in the country is free of it. A report by the National Crime Commission describes it as follows:

> Organized crime ... involves thousands of criminals, working within structures as complex as those of any large corporation, subject to laws more rigidly enforced than those of legitimate governments. Its actions are not impulsive but rather the result of intricate conspiracies, carried on over many years and aimed at gaining control over whole fields of activity in order to amass huge profits. ... Today the core of organized crime in the United States consists of 24 groups operating as criminal cartels in large cities across the Nation.

The report stresses ties between mobsters and corrupt officials:

> All available data indicate that organized crime flourishes only where it has corrupted local officials. As the scope and variety of organized crime's activities have expanded, its need to involve public officials at every level of local government has grown.[42]

The operations of organized crime are most numerous and most effective in the slums. One reason for this is that "escape" through narcotics or gambling is considerably more attractive to people trapped in the ghetto than to those who are better off. Another is that the slum dweller has much less power to make City Hall get rid of the racketeers than do residents of "better" sections. In "respectable" neighborhoods, parents would not stand for organized crime corrupting their children. But ghetto parents have not been able to get effective action against the criminals who have been corrupting ghetto children for years with continuing success. For that matter, middle class parents cannot always prevent their children from seeking in the slum the forbidden pleasures they cannot get near home.

---

42. *The Challenge of Crime in a Free Society: A Report by the President's Commission on Law Enforcement and Administration of Justice* (Washington: February 1967), pp. 187, 192, 191.

EFFECTIVE RACE RIOT CONTROL

As NOTED above, the only way to prevent a race riot is to cure its causes — which isn't a task for the police alone. To eliminate ghettoization, slum housing, school and job discrimination is a job for society as a whole. But while society struggles with these incendiary materials, the police must watch out for blazes and put out any that start. In the present state of American society, racial incidents are a constant possibility, and, as we know only too well by now, a trivial occurrence, if coupled with crowding, heat and humidity, may trigger a major riot.

For this reason, every police department must be prepared to use controlled and disciplined force against possible serious street disorders. The police forces which arrive first on the scene of any outbreak should be the best, most effective and most thoroughly integrated police teams the department can organize. Every effort should be made to insure that major incidents are handled by forces that are overwhelmingly impressive and completely trained, prepared and disciplined. If these standards can be met, almost any problems can be dealt with. But it takes planning; and this cannot be deferred until trouble breaks out. Quick organization and great mobility of substantial forces must be achieved and maintained in advance of trouble.

It is easy to justify these preparations even if they are never used. What the public wants in a fire department is the capacity to put out fires, if any; and if the rigs never have to leave the firehouse, so much the better. A ready police force, capable of moving quickly and effectively, is an essential form of social fire insurance.

Some Case Histories

One of the few available useful analyses of police procedures in race riots compares the Harlem riot of 1943 with the Chicago outbreak of 1919, still one of the worst in American history.[43]

The New York riot took place on an August day in the midst of World War II. It was precipitated by a fight between a Negro soldier and a white policeman. Both were injured, but a rumor spread that the Negro soldier had been shot in the back and killed. Large crowds assembled near the place of the fight.

Mayor Fiorello H. LaGuardia and his police commissioner went to the scene immediately. One-third of the New York police force, from all boroughs, was mobilized and committed to Harlem. The area was cordoned off. The police concentrated on splitting up and dispersing the mob and arresting its leaders. LaGuardia repeatedly addressed Harlem residents on the facts of the situation. Order was restored without the use of firearms.

The report found New York's procedures superior to those employed in Chicago on these four vital counts:

> There was immediate recognition by the police of an unusual and dangerous situation and a quick report to headquarters.
>
> There was a speedy mobilization of the police force, with large reinforcements held in reserve, plus the utilization of civilians as police auxiliaries. Cooperation of neighborhood leaders was enlisted, both to plan strategy and to appeal directly to rioters.
>
> The police were well-trained for the emergency. Rapid, effective steps were taken to prevent curiosity seekers or potential rioters from entering the troubled areas. High civilian officials took over direct command of the efforts to restore order and they stayed on the job until it was finished.
>
> There was no show of prejudice. Special precautions were taken against the excessive use of force and, in addition, there was an insistence on diplomatic and impersonal action on the part of the police officers, as well as an extensive use of Negro policemen and Negro volunteers.[44]

In a recent article, Police Chief Herbert T. Jenkins of Atlanta

---

43. ... *With Justice for All* (Anti-Defamation League of B'nai B'rith and International Association of Chiefs of Police; copyright 1959, 1963), p. 15.
44. *Ibid.*

tells how his city handled four separate riots in 1966 and 1967. In each, prompt mobilization of police and disciplined handling of the rioters quelled disorder with minimal injury and damage.

Chief Jenkins, ascribing the program to Mayor Ivan Allen, Jr., outlined it in this way:

> The City of Atlanta will not slow down in providing equal services for all citizens. There are opportunities for dissent and demonstration by dissatisfied citizens. The city welcomes this, but it must be within the confines of the law.... The city will not be intimidated by the threat of violence, and lawlessness will not be tolerated....
>
> The Atlanta Police have been drilled and trained to avoid what has been termed police brutality and to provide equal protection and service for all citizens and visitors. The police have the authority, under the law, to protect themselves while enforcing the law. The police will not be subjected to being shot at, having bottles and bricks thrown at them, and being spit upon, without taking appropriate action.... The Atlanta Police do not push anyone around, nor will they be pushed around, and will not hesitate to request the assistance of the National Guard if events indicate it necessary....[45]

Detroit: The Riot That Didn't Happen ...

Detroit offers examples of both success and failure in riot control.

On August 9 and 10, 1966, Detroit met a major test. That summer had produced one race riot after another in city after city. Two much smaller Michigan cities had just been severely hit. At this point a routine arrest on Detroit's East Side, for loitering, prompted some young Negroes to call for riot. The resulting crowd quickly grew too big for the precinct officers on or near the scene to handle without additional help.

Police mobilization was prompt. Within an hour there were 200 men on the scene, including a specially trained Tactical Mobile Unit. The area was sealed off; high-ranking officers made a plan for police placement and tactics, and took charge on the scene.

The results of prior intelligence pertaining to riot-prone groups and individuals paid off. Carloads of activists, headed for the area with weapons in their cars, were arrested.

---

45. Herbert T. Jenkins, "Police Challenges and Changes in Atlanta," *The Police Chief,* November 1967, pp. 28, 34.

Where groups formed on the street, the police moved quickly to disperse them. Breaking in, looting and attempted fire bombing were met with prompt arrests.

The Negro community not only refused to rally to the rioters, it moved decisively to cool them off. As word of the trouble spread, leaders of block clubs came to the police station to check on the nature of the disturbances. From there, some went to the trouble spots and urged youngsters to go home. Others telephoned officers of block clubs asking them to get children off the street in their blocks, and to squelch rumors.

Some 150 Negro residents met at a church, pledged their support to the police, and organized two-man citizen "peace patrols" to walk the area. They also set up an information center where residents could check up on rumors.

For two nights, in a relatively small area around Kercheval Avenue, the trouble kept churning. But all it added up to was 43 arrests, some property damage and a few minor injuries. Businesses stayed open. There were no shots fired and no deaths. In short, the riot was not allowed to happen.

... and the One That Did

Another riot broke in Detroit in the early morning hours of Sunday, July 23, 1967. It was triggered by a police raid on a "blind pig" — an illegal after-hours drinking spot. The locale was Twelfth Street, the most explosive in the city; the time was 2:30 a.m. on a hot summer night, in what was the worst summer of racial explosions thus far. The precinct that made the raid had not consulted with, or notified, central police headquarters.

The street reaction was immediate. Saturday night drinkers, pimps, prostitutes and numbers men supplied the active elements in the initial night-time crowds. By dawn many others had arrived on the scene — among them advocates of violent "Black Power" who openly called for riot. Still later, Sunday morning churchgoers added numbers and complications to the Twelfth Street crowd.

Looting of stores on Twelfth Street began before dawn. At 8 a.m. the first fire bombing occurred.

At the time of the initial outbreak, the department was subsequently to reveal, only 193 policemen were on street patrol in the whole city — the lowest coverage in the entire week.

The police's initial response was weak in both manpower and effectiveness. No attempts were made to control the widespread looting. Police efforts concentrated on defending fire units, which came under attack as they arrived. Early in the morning one police squad in wedge formation attempted to regain control of Twelfth Street. A task which a trained force of 100 or more police might have accomplished was undertaken by fewer than 20 officers. The crowd recognized the show of weakness for what it was. No resistance to the progress of the squad was attempted, but rioters dispersed into doorways, alleys and side streets, and flowed back into Twelfth Street after the wedge had passed.

By midmorning the Mobile Task Unit had been partly mobilized. A trained commando platoon under experienced leadership, equipped with tear gas, bayonets and riot guns, was standing by on Twelfth Street.

At the same time, community leaders met at Grace Episcopal Church to seek ways of calming the spreading violence. The meeting decided (with some vigorous dissents) to ask for removal of the commando squad as the price of a civilian attempt to stop the quickly growing riot.

No top administrative city official and no top police administrator was on the scene at that time, nor at any time during the crucial first twelve hours on Sunday.

The civilian leaders, with Congressman John Conyers, Jr., as chief spokesman, attempted to talk to the crowds on Twelfth Street. Conyers made a brave attempt. He was hooted down.

The commando squad was never ordered to clear Twelfth Street. The Mobile Task Unit was "held in reserve" for other emergencies. The word spread on Twelfth Street, and thence through the entire city, that the police were not trying to stop looting. These facts led Detroit's leading Negro newspaper to headline its first post-riot front page "It Could Have Been Stopped."[46]

---

46. *The Michigan Chronicle,* July 29, 1967, p. 1.

Looting now spread far beyond the original riot area. Many persons of usually law-abiding disposition were caught up in the madness. Witnesses subsequently gave vivid descriptions of the carnival atmosphere attending some of the looting. There was ample evidence of anti-white bias in the selection of places to be looted and burned. But there was little or no evidence of any general lynch mob spirit toward white individuals as such. Negro and white looters mingled freely, and white bystanders were generally left unmolested.

But fire bombing spread throughout the city, and fire and police units seeking to respond found themselves under mob attack.

At 2 p.m., eleven and one-half hours after the "blind pig" raid, Mayor Jerome P. Cavanagh called Governor George W. Romney, reported that the rioting was beyond local control, and requested the dispatch of State Troopers and the National Guard.

In the four days that followed, widespread looting, fire bombing and sniping approximated guerrilla warfare conditions in many areas of the city. Of the three major forces involved in suppressing the mass violence, only the 82nd Airborne Division of the United States Army was to emerge with its reputation enhanced. The 82nd arrived late in the riot and was never committed to the worst of the riot areas. But its thorough integration, its cool-headed professional leadership and its completely disciplined response were major factors in ending the violence.

The Detroit Police and the Michigan National Guard bore the brunt of dealing with the worst of the mob violence. The courage and effectiveness of each unit undoubtedly served to restore order and to prevent an even worse holocaust. But in the aftermath of the riot, some actions by personnel of each command were subjected to bitter criticism. Lieutenant General John L. Throckmorton, who commanded the 82nd Airborne and was the ranking military officer on the scene, was later to characterize the National Guard troops as "green" and "trigger-happy." And the *Detroit Free Press* — a paper normally well disposed toward the police — published a lengthy analysis of the 43 riot deaths which plainly implied that a considerable number of them had been unnecessary. Post-riot investigation of the death of three young Negroes in the Algiers Motel resulted in the indictment of two Detroit police officers for murder.

The number of persons killed eventually mounted to 43 — 38 of them civilians. Damage to insured property totaled $38,000,000; uninsured and indirect losses reached still greater proportions.

The riot left a city which had made many vigorous efforts to prevent just this kind of catastrophe reeling from the impact of civic disaster. For days afterwards, troops of the Michigan National Guard and the 82nd Airborne patrolled its streets.

Causes of the Disaster

National news media later emphasized almost unanimously that Detroit's efforts to solve its racial problems had been the most vigorous in the nation, but also that, in the process, the city had developed a complacent attitude of "it can't happen here."

The first of these two observations may be true, but what it principally illustrates is a lack of commitment among other cities to an attack on the problem of the ghetto. As to the second, much of Detroit, official and otherwise, presumably hoped for the best; yet neither public nor private circles doubted that explosive material was present and that the explosion, if it came, could be big.

While Detroit was still burning, *The New York Times* summed up the lessons of the outbreak:

> There are at least two conclusions to be drawn from the tragic events that have condemned forward-looking Detroit to the fate of less-deserving cities.
>
> One is, that if Detroit is an example of America's best efforts to solve the racial and other problems confronting its cities, the best is not nearly good enough.
>
> The other is, that even if progress is achieved on a broad front, the United States must be prepared to contend with serious turbulence in its cities for a long time to come.
>
> As Dr. Kenneth Clark and other sociologists have pointed out, progress in its initial stages tends to generate expectations faster than they can be fulfilled. People who harbor frustrated hopes are more likely to rebel than those with no hope at all.
>
> In this sense, Detroit may be viewed as a victim of its own limited success. But this is no reason to despair or quit. There can be no turning back, even if that were desirable. Detroit's anguish and that of other

American cities will be relieved only when the promising social, economic and educational programs that have been initiated, and additional programs on a huge scale, are pressed to the point where they begin to fulfill the hopes they have rightly engendered.

But meanwhile, the absolute, prime requirement is the restoration of order to the beleaguered city and the application of as much force as is necessary to restore it. Without order there can be no progress.[47]

Three explanations suggest themselves to account for the ferocity and extent of the Detroit riot of 1967. All three are important. All three are also true.

The most fundamental by all odds is society's failure to make the promise of equality for Negroes a reality. America has had 300 years and countless warnings to render equal justice to its Negro citizens. Yet the city of Detroit, the state of Michigan and the United States failed to do enough — in time.

A second, no less important, explanation is that the Detroit Police Department failed to employ its resources promptly enough and firmly enough when the trouble began. In the face of such a holocaust no one can be positive that a different response or tactic would have produced a better result. But if we compare the actual events to what are considered desirable tactics of riot control, the failures of the Police Department are all too obvious:

1. There was a complete failure of prior intelligence.
2. There was a failure to have a sufficient number of men on hand at the outbreak of the riot. (Recognizing that the riot broke at the time of the week when the assigned police manpower was lowest, we must still record this fact.)
3. There was a failure to mobilize quickly enough and to bring reserves into action at the critical moment of the developing riot.
4. There was a failure to apply massive, disciplined and effective force on Twelfth Street at any time during the critical hours—between 2 a.m. and 2 p.m. on the first day.
5. There was a failure to have high-ranking police supervision at the points where critical decisions had to be made in the early hours of the first day, before the riot became general.

---

47. "The Agony of Detroit," *The New York Times*, July 27, 1967, p. 34. Copyright 1967 by The New York Times Company. Reprinted by permission.

Without trying to pinpoint the blame, the absolute least that must be done is to see that such failures of inaction do not recur. While doing so, however, it should be recognized that what is called for is disciplined, intelligent and effective police response. There are, unfortunately, those who would substitute for the indefensible inaction we have discussed an even more indefensible blood bath.

A third explanation of the severity of the disaster is the pattern of fire bombing, which turned a local riot into a city-wide conflagration. There is no hard evidence to prove that the Detroit riot as a whole was planned — either at the Kremlin in Moscow or at the Black Power Conference in Newark. And the way it actually started argues strongly against any prior plan as to timing. But Black Power activists did move into the riot in its early stage to intensify and to spread it. As noted in an earlier chapter, there is considerable reason to believe that at least part of the attendant havoc in the Cincinnati, Newark and Detroit outbreaks of 1967 was planned and organized. Indeed, it is possible that planned fire bombing was the added factor which put the Detroit riot of 1967 out of control and justified the term "rebellion" later applied to it by Black Power extremists.

The indications of planning are certainly sufficient to highlight the great need for prior police intelligence work. They also serve to highlight what a tragedy it is that Detroit has substantially dismantled its police intelligence unit — not many years ago regarded as one of the best in the nation.

Recommended Control Methods

A generally authoritative publication on riot control was distributed nationwide to local law enforcement officials by the Federal Bureau of Investigation in the spring of 1967.[48] This booklet deals in depth with appropriate police training, intelligence work and planning prior to outbreaks of violence. It includes recommendations for alerting and seeking aid from state and national authorities if a disturbance exceeds local control.

---

48. *Prevention and Control of Mobs and Riots* (Federal Bureau of Investigation, U.S. Department of Justice, April 3. 1967), pp. 87-94.

We shall quote from two sections directly relevant to riot control by local police.

At the outset, according to the FBI, the police commander's best bet is a purposeful, disciplined display of force and a resolve to convince the mob that the police can and will maintain law and order — if necessary by force.

> The next step is for the police commander to give the order to disperse; such an order should not be given until the commander has sufficient force to back up his order. Never bluff! Officers who participate in a show of force must be well disciplined so they will follow orders to the letter, stand firm in the face of abuse, and not lose their heads.

If the more law-abiding of the citizens momentarily caught up in the mob do not yield to a show of force, they may yield to actual force. Such action should be kept to the minimum necessary at any given moment, since unwarranted application of force may incite a mob to further violence. Depending on the need, force may be gradually intensified:

> Applying force by degrees insures that the maximum force employed to restore order is applied to the most violent and lawless individuals only. The degrees and the order of the application of force should be decided in advance.... All officers involved in the operation must be aware of these degrees and must know when each is to be applied and by whose authority. This is not meant to imply that police should not meet force with greater force; it does mean that unnecessary bloodshed must be avoided whenever possible.

Priorities in the use of force will depend on available weapons and equipment. Tear gas can serve to prevent threatened violence by rioters or to disperse them. When chemicals are used, there must be an avenue of escape; otherwise panic may result.

> Chemical agents, properly employed ... can negate the numerical superiority the mob has over the police force. They are the most effective and most humane means of achieving temporary neutralization of a mob with a minimum of personal injury. Chemical agents should not be used or threatened to disperse demonstrators who are not in fact endangering public safety and security.

The baton, the FBI warns, must be judiciously used to be effective without inflicting unnecessary injury. Officers must be thoroughly trained in its use.

The baton should be used only in an emergency, and when blows are struck, it should be with the intention of stunning or temporarily disabling, rather than inflicting injury. Blows to the head should be avoided. The baton used as an extension of the arm is generally more effective than when used as a bludgeon or club.

The armed forces' order of priorities might serve as a model, the FBI suggests:

1. Unloaded rifles with bayonets fixed and sheathed.
2. Unloaded rifles with bare bayonets fixed.
3. Tear gas (CS and CN).
4. Loaded rifles with bare bayonets fixed.

The FBI recommendations emphasize that firearms are to be used only as a last resort:

> The decision to resort to the use of firearms is indeed a grave one.... Among the important considerations, of course, are the protection of the officer's own life, as well as the lives of fellow officers, and the protection of innocent citizens. A basic rule in police firearms training is that a firearm is used only in self-defense or to protect the lives of others.

Officers should never fire indiscriminately into a crowd, the FBI stresses, lest they injure or kill innocent persons and thereby provoke a worse clash. Nor should they fire over the heads of crowds — a bluffing technique which may defeat itself or may take lives unnecessarily through poorly aimed or ricocheting bullets.

Snipers must be quickly and severely dealt with, the FBI recommendations continue, both because they pin down the police and because they endanger human lives.

> It may be necessary to employ a countersniper, equipped and trained in the use of high-powered, telescopic-equipped rifles. Police officers, crouched behind any means of protection available and firing their service revolvers or shotguns aimlessly at a building or rooftop, are endangering lives and, at the same time, are prevented from accomplishing their mission.

As for other weapons, the bayonet can be an effective deterrent — used, not as a night stick or baton, but with the standard shotgun, especially in shows of force and standard riot control formations.

CHANNELS OF COMMUNICATION

PEOPLE WHO KNOW (or believe) that they are denied access to any crucial government agency are easy prey for advocates of lawlessness. Therefore, one essential in resolving or preventing conflict between the police and the public is communication. The police must be willing to listen to citizens' opinions, suggestions and, particularly, complaints. What is more, citizen support for the work of the police must be actively solicited.

Organizing for Day-to-Day Communication

Police administrations must open and maintain contact with all sections of the communities they serve — particularly, in this decade, with Negro citizens. Police departments should be ready at all times to meet with communal leaders, to exchange information with them and to tackle issues together. If the department is conscious of a particular problem, it should not wait for someone to call, but should initiate discussions.

After one riot situation, a newly appointed Police Commissioner[49] managed to gain the confidence of the thoroughly disaffected Negro population. His method was not particularly dramatic: He simply attended every public meeting of any importance in the Negro community. Because he made himself easily accessible, rumors were reported and checked quickly; justified complaints could be dealt with promptly and effectively.

Still, this kind of individual performance under crisis condi-

---

49. John Ballenger, who was appointed Police Commissioner of Detroit on the heels of the 1943 riot.

tions is no substitute for systematizing the entire range of day-in, day-out communications. Though communication starts in the mayor's and the police commissioner's (or police chief's) office, it reaches what is perhaps its most significant phase in confrontations on the street. Therefore, the whole city and the whole police department must be involved.

At the top level, the mayor's office, the city council and the human relations commission should be easily accessible, as should be the office of the police chief and the police complaint bureau.

In each precinct, the police captain or inspector should be on a first-name basis with the principals of high schools and junior high schools. He should know the priests, ministers and rabbis of the larger congregations, as well as the directors of every social agency located or active in the area. Policemen often are dubious or indifferent when such contacts are first officially required; but the results usually convince even the most skeptical old-timer.

"Open house" should be held regularly in each precinct, preferably in the station house, at least once every quarter. A high-ranking officer of the Department should be present. There should be a program dealing with the work of the police, followed by ample opportunity for airing complaints with the precinct commander or the visiting officer.

In addition, precincts should encourage block clubs, P.T.A.s and neighborhood associations to discuss law enforcement problems at their meetings. Precinct lieutenants and sergeants should be assigned to attend such meetings as often as other duties allow.

In the last few years, a number of cities have encouraged community efforts of this sort. The programs are often carried out in cooperation with designated human relations officers on the police force. In Chicago, neighborhood leaders now join with police human relations specialists in monthly "community workshops," reviewing not only law enforcement problems, but also complaints against other city agencies, which the police relay to the appropriate department. Neighborhood advisory committees or voluntary community councils of this sort are operating in St. Louis, Philadelphia, New York and elsewhere. In Baltimore, members of an integrated community relations unit within the police department work on a day-to-day basis with civil rights organizations, and meet periodically with teen-age groups to "defuse" troubles. Contacts like these can do much to weaken the picture of the police department as an occupying enemy force.

Special Situations

How to communicate with hostile meetings or potentially explosive demonstrations is a special problem. In this connection, it is important to remember that most citizens will be pleased — and some may be pleasantly surprised — by a police visit that is cooperative and courteous. This fact is of tremendous importance even in coping with openly antagonistic groups.

In 1962, Elijah Muhammad and Malcolm X, the two black nationalist leaders — then on the warmest of terms with each other — held a nationwide rally in one city to protest actions in another part of the country. The local Police Department set up the usual conferences with the sponsors of the rally to arrange for parking and traffic handling. The spirit in which these routine talks were held measurably decreased the chances of violence. The preparations even resulted in unsolicited praise for the local police from the platform of the protest meeting.

The next year, a big freedom march took place in the same city. The parade permit was issued at the Police Department's recommendation. The police subsequently took extensive part in planning the parade route, gathering places, timing and other details. The planning was actually done at meetings of the Parade Marshals in the board room at police headquarters. The huge affair went off in peace and order.

Communication with the public is not only a valuable means of preventing trouble; it can also be useful in preparing for trouble that is bound to arise. It is important to make the public understand in advance that if force is ever needed it will be applied in a competent, disciplined way — to build and maintain a reputation for alertness and capability in dealing with violence.

This advance communications job is best done as a routine

affair on neutral occasions, such as public practice exercises or police parades. The time to do it is not when political demonstrations or protest meetings actually take place. To display excessive force at a rally that is peaceful in intent can be more provocative than helpful. On occasions of that kind, the police should figure as an agency for serving, not curbing, the public — and should make this purpose clear by the bearing of the police officers on hand, the equipment they carry, and the numbers assigned to routine tasks like traffic handling.

Evaluating Citizens' Complaints

Honest and effective investigation of civilian complaints, together with appropriate correction, is essential to any sound police-community relations program.

The first requirement is to find the facts and face them. This has not always been the practice. "The police officer is always right" is a familiar slogan in precinct stations, and policemen often yield to the temptation to conceal conduct which violates the law and the book of procedure. For example, a police report may state that four officers brought in a prisoner with a four-inch cut on the top of his head, caused by "falling on the precinct steps." Just how he contrived to fall on the top of his head while being marched up the steps is not explained, nor why four officers should have been unable to bring him in undamaged.

On the other hand, facts also can be misstated to the disadvantage of the police. An offender arrested for good cause naturally would like to find something that will discredit the officer who arrests him. He may very well tell lies to do so. Some skepticism is appropriate in judging his story.

There are, of course, facts which no amount of investigation can accurately determine. If a belligerent drunk takes a swing at an officer, no one can scientifically calculate afterwards whether the pounds of pressure which the officer exerted in return, by fist or billy, were the least amount of force needed to subdue the drunk. Again, a police officer who knows that his own life is in jeopardy has both the legal right and the duty to protect himself by every reasonable means. Thus, a degree of basic discretion is of necessity vested in the officer.

But most situations can be more precisely evaluated. As pointed out earlier, most events on city streets are seen by a number of people. If a careful inquiry is made, and the statements of those who were on the scene are recorded, the chances are that a pretty accurate picture of the incident will emerge.

Vincent W. Piersante, then Detroit's Chief of Detectives, speaking at the 1965 Convention of the Michigan Association of Chiefs of Police, had this to say about handling infractions of police rules:

> We in law enforcement must demonstrate our willingness and ability to take proper action against members of our force when they violate the rules and regulations or the law.
>
> This does not mean that every infraction made by a police officer is a hanging offense, or requires discharge. We deal with difficult and complicated problems—our men must make decisions in the heat of combat, and based on their beliefs at the time of the action. And if the officer's judgment, though poor, was not motivated by greed or prejudice, the correction could be merely further instruction or a reprimand. The correction, in any case, should be commensurate with the infraction. (Disciplinary action, if any, must be based on the just determination of the facts, and enforcement officials must have the courage to withstand internal and external pressures, and do what is just.) If the officer deserves correction, he should have it—as we would expect it in any other function of government, or any other walk of life.

Chief Piersante went on to stress that nothing less than complete candor would do:

> Any situation where the truth is allowed to be covered up by official reports is productive of the greatest amount of hostility and disregard for law. A belief that the truth is being glossed over is a major source of problems in the area of which we are speaking. . . .
>
> This may sound like preemption of our function as police officials—but we must remember that we are now in the process of attempting to overcome the sins of commission and omission of enforcement that for decades have been accepted as a way of life by a minority segment of our population.

Inside vs. Outside Civilian Review

Effective civilian control of police departments is as essential to the survival of democracy as is civilian control of military forces. The disposition of important citizen complaints should be controlled by the civilian head of the police. The reports of the police's community relations bureau should go directly to him.

The community relations bureau, for its part, should be as nearly pressure-proof as possible. It should not consist of line officers — that is, officers within the chain of command — because they are too vulnerable to broad hints from above and resentments from below. Instead, it should be manned by staff officers — administrative specialists responsible directly to the top — who can afford to take a wholly honest stand.

At a meeting not long ago, a command officer from a major police department who was describing the elaborate complaint investigation system of his force was asked whether line or staff officers handled the street investigations. He replied, "Line officers." When it was pointed out privately that under this procedure the investigating officer would be reporting on a brother officer with whom he might shortly again be working as a partner, the speaker promptly acknowledged that this system could not really be expected to produce unbiased reports. But, he said, the men on the force would not stand for staff investigation — which means that the police command had little real control over discipline.

It is this sort of inadequacy which has produced the nationwide demands for outside civilian review boards. Where the civilian authority in charge of the police abdicates its duty to govern the practices of the force, an outside review board strikes citizens as a plausible alternative.

Such boards, however, have many defects. Two American cities, Philadelphia and Rochester, have had civilian review boards, and both underwent major riots — which suggests that the outside board is no panacea. Neither board, it should be noted, had an adequate investigative staff of its own, and neither had any control over whatever remedial measures were found desirable.

In the spring of 1966, when controversy over a proposed outside review board in New York City was running high, an analysis in *The New York Times* appraised the issue as follows:

> ... Most policemen view the board as a kangaroo court that will callously toss them into the river in order to satisfy the politically potent racial minorities.
>
> On the other hand, a number of civil rights leaders, having pitched the issue as though it were a second Magna Carta, are now expressing bitterness over the plan's structural inadequacies and personal makeup.
>
> But responsible, sophisticated people on both sides of the fence have long recognized . . . that a review board, no matter how constituted, is highly unlikely to justify police nightmares or minority-group dreams.
>
> ... The reasoning behind this feeling is rooted in experience, human nature, and the institutional limitations of review boards to curb brutal or uncouth police tactics.
>
> ... Even if the civilian board could make recommendations of punishment, experience in other cities shows that they would not be very tough on the policemen.
>
> Thus, the Philadelphia review board, which is entirely civilian, has been easier on the boys in blue than New York's all-police board, which has been in operation since 1953.[50]

In my opinion, outside review boards are bad in principle for both the citizens and the police. It is bad government to separate authority from responsibility. Fair control over police practices by civilians inside the department may be difficult to establish, but once established, it can produce both vigorous and equal law enforcement. No outside review board can really produce either.

The Ombudsman Plan

Another widely discussed method of reviewing police actions is the appointment of an official "public protector" or guardian of the people's rights, whose job would be to receive complaints about unfair actions or malfunctions by any government agency, investigate the complaints and bring proceedings against the erring officials. In Sweden, where this system is well established, this officer

---

50. Sidney E. Zion, "Civilian Review Board Will Be No Panacea," *The New York Times*, May 8, 1966, section 4, p. 5. Copyright 1966 by The New York Times Company. Reprinted by permission.

is called *ombudsman* ("representative"). Denmark and New Zealand also have ombudsmen.

In the United States, an aggrieved citizen can now turn to the courts for legal redress against government abuses, but this procedure is likely to be slow, expensive and, to many citizens, frightening. Or he can write to his Congressman. This will sometimes get results, but often it will not, for Congressmen are overloaded with such "case work." An ombudsman allegedly would provide surer and faster redress; and where the complainant does not have a case, he would supply a reasonable explanation. According to its advocates, the system does much to increase people's confidence in their government.

Whether the idea can be made to work in this country remains to be seen. It is favored by Negro organizations, religious groups and some spokesmen for police associations in such cities as New York, but so far it is being tried only on a minute scale. A start has been made in Nassau County, New York, where a Commissioner of Accounts acts as public protector for citizens in their dealings with the county and its subdivisions. Ombudsmen-like powers in relation to race discrimination complaints have been given to the Civil Rights Commission of the State of Michigan.

Meanwhile, bills to establish ombudsmen's offices are pending in several state legislatures. It is at least possible that some such plan may prove useful in dealing with police-community relations, as well as other of our society's problems.

ORGANIZING CITIZEN SUPPORT

CITIZENS have a tremendous stake in how their police department operates. They should be eager to support it in the proper discharge of its duties. They should be willing to get involved. But are they?

In 1964, a woman named Kitty Genovese was murdered in the Queens section of New York City within sight or hearing of 38 people. Not one called the police. They didn't want to get involved.

In 1965, in Detroit, a police officer desperately struggled to prevent a would-be suicide from throwing himself off an expressway bridge. When the officer asked for help in trying to lift the man to safety, one citizen lent a hand. Hundred of others passed by, not wanting to be involved.

These are sad commentaries on our civilization.

Citizen backing for law enforcement is a necessity in a democratic society. With it, the police can act as the community's right arm in fighting the city's evils. Without it, the police tend to become an alien force imposing its power on a resentful population.

This means, on one hand, that the police must actively solicit the community's support, and on the other that the community must take some initiatives toward furnishing it. Both steps are particularly essential among traditionally hostile minority groups.

Police Initiatives

To date, the police have rarely sought civilian assistance — least of all in those areas where the forces of the law have been hardest pressed. Yet, as noted earlier, the great majority of residents in these areas, just as in others, are law-abiding. Thus, chances of obtaining citizen support for genuine efforts to curb crime are much better in such neighborhoods than people generally realize.

Roy Wilkins, Executive Director of the National Association for the Advancement of Colored People, recently emphasized the Negro community's increasing willingness to support vigorous law enforcement:

> Negro law violators enjoyed a sort of racial brotherhood status, not because all other Negroes were criminally inclined, but because black men have had such a "hard way to go" that other black men nearly always gave them a break against law officers. . . .
>
> The real news is that a part of the Negro community is now ready to blow the whistle on the robbers, muggers and knife men. It still works in many places (even in Harlem), but apparently the days of the black skin distress signal are numbered. Crime control becomes a real possibility as soon as the law-abiding Negro citizens, always in the vast majority, take an active, rather than a passive, role against crime and criminals.[51]

In 1962, the Detroit Police Department published a Citizens' Law Enforcement Code, suggesting ten ways in which citizens could help make their own communities safer:

1. If you see a fight, an accident, a crime, call WO 2-5700 and state the facts to the police officer who answers.
2. If you see circumstances which make you believe a holdup, a burglary, or other violent crime is being committed, call WO 2-5700 and state what you have seen and the location to the police officer who answers.
3. If you know where organized crime is operating in gambling, in sale of narcotics, or in vice, call or write the Inspector of your precinct or the Commissioner or Superintendent of Police. . . .
4. Help us protect your property. Lock your car. Lock your door.
5. If you receive a ticket for an inadvertent violation of a traffic ordinance, accept it as a reminder which could save a life. The police department emphasizes police courtesy. Citizen courtesy helps, too.
6. Sound law enforcement depends on citizen support. Be willing to give your name as a witness. Be prepared to testify in court.
7. Rely on the police department for protection. Never carry weapons. Teach children not to carry knives. Keep guns away from children.
8. Teach your children to respect our law and to regard the police officer as a guardian and a friend.

---

51. Roy Wilkins, "A New Look at Crime," *New York Post*, March 13, 1966. Reprinted by permission of the Register & Tribune Syndicate.

9. Set an example for your children of living by the moral code of your religious faith. Give them convictions strong enough to resist a temptation or a dare to do what they know is wrong.
10. Be proud "to get involved" in supporting law enforcement.

Chicago, one of the cities plagued most by crime problems and racial tensions, has seen real progress as a result of a similar plan. Under Orlando W. Wilson's leadership, the Police Department has actively sought citizen help — and found it. For example, at the police's invitation, grass-roots civic leaders have taken part in a week-long seminar on police-community relations at Michigan State University, together with the community service specialists whom the department maintains in each of the city's 20 districts.[52]

It is well to warn the public in advance that increased citizen support will, if successful, seemingly increase the prevalence of crime, because more crimes will be reported by citizens and recorded by the police. The difference probably will not be great where homicide and automobile theft are concerned; these crimes are usually reported anyway because murder is considered serious by everyone, and car thefts involve people's self-interest. But other crimes will be recorded much more frequently once the campaign hits its stride. More of what might be called the iceberg of crime — the volume of unreported crime referred to by the National Crime Commission[53] — will be exposed to public view.

A Case History

What a campaign to involve citizens in law enforcement can accomplish was recently described in a *Wall Street Journal* account of "Operation Friend," a program in New York's 24th Precinct:

> Police in a turbulent portion of Manhattan's west side are building bridges to the Puerto Rican community with an effort combining education, imagination and a dash of sociology.
>
> Operation Friend, as it is called, has produced everything from kite-flying contests for children to seminars for their elders to classes in Puerto Rican mores for the policemen.

---

52. "Chicago Stresses Riot Prevention," *The New York Times*, June 5, 1967, p. 49.
53. *The Challenge of Crime in a Free Society, op. cit.*, pp. 20, 21, 22.

Friction between the Spanish-speaking newcomers and the establishment represented most visibly by the policeman has been a continuing problem for New York City. Operation Friend cuts two ways: Persuading the citizenry that policemen are human—and humane—servants of the public; and persuading policemen that they can win the backing of the community, and function better with it.

One part of "Operation Friend" has been to form a community council with hundreds of members, representing every block in the area. These individuals serve as contacts in crisis. In one instance, thanks to this system, a community council representative succeeded in keeping a crowd of angry people from attacking a policeman they mistakenly thought responsible for an eviction. But there is more to "Operation Friend" than that.

> The Puerto Rican, struggling for survival in a frequently hostile environment, tended to identify the man in blue with his frustration.
>
> The police decided to meet the Puerto Ricans half way. Teachers from the Board of Education went to the 24th precinct and held classes in Spanish. Like a merchant who learns the language to sell his wares, the men of the 24th are learning to communicate.
>
> Every man on the beat has an English-Spanish handbook. . . .
>
> The thrice-weekly training sessions held for policemen of the 24th on police matters now include instruction on Puerto Rican mores and habits.

At the same time, the police in the area are trying to gain the understanding of the public. Literature, in Spanish, is available to inform citizens of the police's many unsung services — such as delivering babies in emergencies, keeping innocent people from harm, and reporting building violations by landlords.

For children, the precinct has put out a comic book, *The Policeman Is Your Friend*. In other ways, too, young people are being reached and befriended:

> Policemen have taken busloads of youngsters to museums, the Hayden Planetarium, local beaches and to Washington, D.C. . . . Last February 39 children and a contingent of policemen went to a camp at Rifton, N.Y. for a winter excursion. They held snow-ball fights, went sleigh-riding, and even toasted marshmallows together.

A small foundation grant made it possible for 11 policemen

from the area to spend two weeks in Puerto Rico with local families, so as to gain an insight into the problems and frustrations facing the Puerto Rican who comes to New York. In part because of this experience, the officer's initial skepticism and cynicism about the program has evaporated.

According to Ralph Rojas, Director of the New York office of the Commonwealth of Puerto Rico Migration Division, the Puerto Rican community is swinging behind the program, and the general community is benefiting also. The article concludes:

> The picture isn't all hearts and flowers. Far from it. The 24th precinct is only one section of the city. The perennial problems of drug addiction and crime continue. There still are policemen convinced that a night stick is the best persuader, and Puerto Ricans convinced that the policeman is their worst enemy. But Operation Friend has improved the climate of relations....[54]

Community Initiatives

American visitors have often been struck by the respect and confidence accorded to the policeman in England. For over a century, the British "bobby," as he is affectionately nicknamed, has gone about with a night stick as his only weapon; yet in the 20 years between the First and the Second World War only one police officer was killed in the entire country. Though unarmed, the "bobby" is feared by criminals — in large part because the public almost invariably comes to his aid. A highly placed former police official described the British public's attitude thus:

> We in England conceive the suppression of crime as the job of the people and the police alike. We accept the fact that the police act for the people. ... We gave our police the status and dignity befitting their important role as public protectors.

If all Americans were to adopt a similar attitude toward their police, it would make a big dent in the law enforcement problems that plague the nation. Citizens, both black and white, have had

---

54. Bowen Northrup, "Operation Friend," *The Wall Street Journal*, August 2, 1966, p. 14.

cause to complain about the policeman's insensitivity to some of their concerns; but in turn they have shown little awareness of the policeman's responsibilities and little inclination to help him.

What, then, can citizens do to build a two-way street of understanding and support between themselves and police?

GREATER INVOLVEMENT WITH LAW ENFORCEMENT. One effective step citizens can take is simply to help support law enforcement in the neighborhood. Too many people still feel that whoever cooperates with the police is a traitor, or is getting "unnecessarily involved." It is time for all citizens to place themselves unequivocally on the side of law and order — and to let the police know it. To the individual, this means things as elementary as reporting instead of ignoring criminal acts, such as that which took the life of Kitty Genovese. To grass-roots organizations it may mean setting up new working relationships with the police — to serve as two-way channels by which citizens can effectively present problems and complaints to the police, and the police can enlist the public's aid in fighting crime.

Citizens and citizen groups have at times greatly aided the police in preventing or quelling disturbances. For example, during outbreaks at Tampa and Dayton, in 1967, Negro youths formed emergency patrols that did yeoman service in persuading rioters to go home. Similarly, responsible members of the public have helped dispel inflammatory rumors and kept crowds from building up in times of tension.

BACK POLICE NEEDS. At the city or regional level, citizen groups and opinion molders can improve law enforcement by helping the police get what they need to do a first-rate job — enough manpower, adequate facilities, up-to-date instruction, or salaries competitive with those paid elsewhere. (Two years after Watts, a Negro newspaper in Los Angeles firmly endorsed a bond issue that would provide for better police training, new station houses and modern equipment.)

REACHING THE YOUNG. A particularly crucial issue is the relationship between police and young people. Recent studies find that adolescents — not only in the ghetto but also among the middle class — tend to be extremely hostile to police, and that this hostility as often as not stems from unpleasant contacts with individual policemen. Since a huge percentage of crimes is committed by boys and girls under 20, this widespread animosity is a major threat to law and order.

Citizens can help by supporting police efforts to create better relationships — through the traditional Police Athletic Leagues as well as through undertakings like New York's "Operation Friend," Cincinnati's annual young people's march and reception at police stations on Law Day, and Chicago's "Officer Friendly" program for small children. Community organizations should ask the police and the schools in their own interest to institute such programs and should help operate them.

Public support is needed, not only for "get-acquainted" programs like these, but also for newly developing police apprenticeship programs. In some cities, "cadet" positions are now offered high-school boys, recent graduates or dropouts — partly to help build better attitudes, partly to encourage young men to make the police their career. In St. Louis, for example, a pre-police program for 14- and 15-year-olds is partly financed by businessmen and conducted with the help of the YMCA.

Cadet programs obviously benefit police departments, which are having much trouble in recruiting. But they are equally beneficial to minority groups, who have always been underrepresented or unrepresented on police forces, and can now rectify the balance through this avenue. Since integration of police forces is in the interest of Negroes and other minorities, civil rights groups naturally will collaborate with police cadet programs, or demand to have them instituted where they do not yet exist. They can also organize courses to help interested young people prepare themselves for the examination they must pass to join the force.

DISPELLING WARPED IMAGES. The community can help to dispel the distorted images of the police in the minds of many citizens. Today, the man in the street often thinks of the police officer in connection with things that are bad, rarely with things that are good. But there is no reason why neighborhoods should not reach out to involve police much more than is customary today in matters involving local pride, such as charitable causes, clean-block campaigns, graduation ceremonies or block parties. And there is no reason why neighborhoods, rather than just city officials, should not accord public recognition to outstandingly helpful or courageous police officers.

A special responsibility, both to the police and the public, lies with those who disseminate the news. Newspaper, radio and television often exaggerate, or give undue prominence, to violence and community tensions, on the theory that bad news is more interesting than good. Minor incidents are sometimes presented as riots; normal and necessary force is sometimes made to appear to be brutality. Stories of progress and good will are often played down or ignored. This sort of caricaturing is particularly dangerous on TV, because TV reporting has a way of raising temperatures both among those whom it shows on the screen and among the viewers. There is little doubt that lurid reporting can provoke trouble. For this reason, newsmen's associations, schools of journalism, police departments and other responsible groups have begun to draw up local codes defining what is proper reporting in times of crisis, and what is inflammatory. Wherever irresponsible reporting persists, citizens should press for adoption of such standards.

HOW BUSINESS CAN HELP. The business community, too, can play a special role in minimizing the causes of tension, particularly during the "long, hot summers." In New York, Philadelphia, Cleveland, Detroit and other large cities, business organizations, large and small, have taken concerted action to provide summer employment and job training for ghetto youngsters — training that will bear fruit the year round. Some have also financed a variety of employment and recreational programs, as an antidote to the idleness and boredom that underlie so much of the ghetto's summertime troubles.

MAKE SUPPORT KNOWN. And finally, citizens at all times need to keep the policeman aware that they are with him. Police departments and policemen's organizations should know that citizen groups are ready to work with them for common objectives. In many communities today, police officers feel constantly threatened and on the defensive; and when responsible citizens or citizen groups — including civil rights groups — fail to assure them of their support, irresponsible ones rush in to fill the vacuum. In some cities, extremist groups like the John Birch Society have gained undue influence among police officers, simply by pre-empting the slogan, "Support Your Local Police." Order is everybody's business, and support for it should not be the exclusive prerogative of the most reactionary element in the community.

TOWARD A 20th-CENTURY POLICE FORCE

THIS PAMPHLET has outlined how relations between the police and the public, particularly the Negro public in big cities, can be modernized and improved for the sake of better law enforcement, including the control of disturbances. Improvements on the order of those outlined here will require two kinds of major change in the nature of the police operation during the next few years. First, police departments need to be racially integrated far more thoroughly than most of them are now. And second, police forces will have to be larger, better trained, better financed and better paid.

The majority of police officers will welcome these changes. They want no part of old inadequacies and abuses. It may be hoped that citizens and their governments will also support the needed improvements — financially and otherwise.

Integrating the Force

Perhaps nothing will do more in the long run to give Negroes confidence in the police than the presence of black faces on the force. People believe what they see. An integrated scout car or an integrated police detachment proclaims fair and authoritative law enforcement; the absence of integration suggests the opposite.

The percentage of Negroes among policemen has always been low, and still is. For many years, it was exceedingly difficult for qualified Negroes to get on the police force. In recent years, the problem has shifted; it is now exceedingly difficult for police forces to attract qualified Negroes, though many are trying hard.

The competition for potentially qualified men is intense. Young Negro high-school graduates with an I.Q. of 100 or more are now being keenly sought after in the job market, and they may find other jobs more desirable. Besides, the potential Negro police recruit senses he is likely to face hostility in his home community if he puts on the blue coat; and he anticipates animosity from some people with the police department. These circumstances, combined with the past history of discrimination in the field, are often sufficient to keep him away, even though he may be eligible for the force and interested in joining it.

In short, tearing down barriers to employment is not enough. What is needed is a positive effort to inspire young Negroes to seek police work — much as thousands of young people have been inspired to join the Peace Corps, or to seek careers in teaching, social work or industry.

The "police cadet" programs mentioned earlier are one possible approach. Vigorous, continuing recruitment campaigns addressed specifically to Negroes are another. Such campaigns could enlist the aid of newspapers, radio and television, of ministers, community leaders, and organizations like the Urban League and the National Association for the Advancement of Colored People. New York City has shown considerable ingenuity in conducting targeted recruiting campaigns; Negroes and Puerto Ricans there are reached, not only in high schools and colleges, but also at armed forces separation centers and even at beaches, movies and ball games.

At the same time, measures must be taken to insure — and to make it obvious — that advancement is equally open to all in police work. The unwritten color lines in police administration die hard. For example, as of 1962 no Negro police officer in Detroit had ever advanced to the rank of uniformed lieutenant; there were many units in the department where not a single Negro officer had ever served. A similar indefensible state of affairs still prevails in many cities, and in almost all, integration of police details has been strongly resisted. But the practical value, as well as the legal and moral correctness of integrated forces, is gradually being recognized. The old obstacles can be overcome by careful, determined administrative planning.

In New York, Los Angeles and St. Louis, applicants for police jobs are enrolled in courses that will increase their chances of passing the examinations. Similar pre-training programs were recently under consideration in such cities as Baltimore, Cincinnati and Cleveland. The courses are financed by the U.S. Department of Labor, with Manpower Development and Training Act funds. Of course, they are not limited to minority groups. But most of the trainees come from Negro, Puerto Rican or Mexican-American neighborhoods. In mid-1967, 70 per cent of the participants in the New York program were Negroes or Puerto Ricans.

Higher Standards and Status

Though city police officers are the front line of law enforcement, the community pays them badly, assigns them a relatively low social status and appreciates them only in moments of emergency. Faced with such attitudes, the police are not always able to do an acceptable job, and they certainly will not be able to meet current demands for higher standards of performance.

Our goal must be to have our streets policed by men recruited, trained and paid at professional levels. One model could be the Federal Bureau of Investigation, which has built an enviable reputation for following the law while enforcing it. The FBI's professional standards are much higher than those of metropolitan police forces today; its case load is proportionately much smaller. Both of these objectives should be sought for local law enforcement.

While law enforcement is likely to remain a local responsibility for the foreseeable future, there is no reason why Federal assistance should not be sought for police needs. In Great Britain, where the national government has participated for many years in financing local police, performance is not only considerably more uniform than in the United States, but probably also somewhat more professional.

Chief Jenkins, of the Atlanta Police Department, has convincingly argued the case for Federal aid:

> I look forward to the day when the U.S. Justice Department and the U.S. Congress will say to every city police department, regardless of its size: "If your department meets all the professional standards in police re-

cruitment, police pay, police training, and police supervision, the federal government will contribute a percentage of your annual budget — it should be about 50 per cent."[55]

Chief Jenkins is not frightened by the possibility of a national police force. Most local police effort goes into enforcing Federal laws anyway, he points out, so that some degree of Federal control and procedure must be accepted. In any case, he emphasizes, only the combined best efforts of Federal, state and local government can meet the mounting cost of law enforcement and stem the rising tide of crime.

Better training will account for much of the added cost. In the not too distant future, at least two years of college should be required for police careers. A fully trained and qualified police officer should command a salary around $10,000 a year. (In 1966, according to the *Municipal Yearbook,* the median salary of policemen in cities over 25,000 was $5,843; in cities between 10,000 and 25,000, it was $4,920.)

So far, formal college-level training specifically for police officers is still a rarity, though New York City has made a start with its College of Police Science, a branch of the City University, and Michigan State University's Police Administration School is another of a number of pioneer efforts in this field. Consideration should be given to a National Police College — a four-year, degree-granting institution organized, staffed and financed somewhat like West Point. Qualified young men who are prepared to commit themselves to law enforcement careers should be appointed to this school at no cost to themselves. They might be drawn from local law enforcement ranks, or from the ranks of high-school graduates. A National Police College would supply a corps of professional police officers highly qualified to fill local police leadership posts in future decades.

Intergroup relations will figure increasingly in the training of tomorrow's policemen, for no officer can work smoothly with his

---

55. Jenkins, *op. cit.,* pp. 28, 30-31.

particular public unless he understands that public's special problems, its attitudes and sensitive spots, its history, folkways and forms of organization.

Intergroup training of police offers private groups an opportunity to make a significant contribution. A large-scale program in Philadelphia is sponsored by a citizens' organization, the Philadelphia Fellowship Commission; a similar one in Detroit is financed by the Ford Foundation; several seminars on police-community relations were sponsored jointly by the New York Police Department and the American Jewish Committee. In the future, such cooperation might profitably become the rule everywhere.

In the next few decades we will need, not only better-trained police officers, but also more — probably many more. One reason is the impact, still increasing, of the problems of urbanization and migration. Another is the higher standards of performance demanded by court rulings like those in the *Mapp* and *Miranda* cases. Old methods like the "third degree" and raids without warrant are economical of police man-hours; but they are repugnant to American ideals of justice.

To date, we have accepted a standard of 2.5 police officers per 1,000 population, and rarely achieved even that. Tomorrow, we may need to raise the standard to 3.5 per 1,000, and achieve it.

The cost of such a manpower increase, and of the other improvements suggested here, is great. But if we can pay the bills involved in beating the Soviet Union to the moon, we should be able to pay what it costs to make our streets safe to walk on.

Single copy, $1.00
Quantity prices on request

Don't miss *these important companion pamphlets:*

■ CRIME AND RACE
Conceptions and Misconceptions

> BY MARVIN E. WOLFGANG   A noted sociologist's analysis of facts and fallacies underlying crime statistics, of vital interest to law enforcement officers, criminologists and intergroup workers. *Crime and Race* examines the FBI "crime index" and other records, and draws some startling conclusions about effects of race prejudice in shaping public thinking about criminality.   **50¢**

■ CASE STUDY OF A RIOT
The Philadelphia Story

> BY LENORA E. BERSON   An incisive analysis of the racial explosion that shook one city — and a clear picture of conditions and festering resentments just below the surface in other Negro communities where "the normalcy of the ghetto is still squalor, ignorance, disease and deprivation; still slum housing at high rent; still inferior education; still chronic unemployment."   **75¢**

■ THE POLICE AND RACE RELATIONS
A Selected Bibliography

> A handy listing of nearly 100 books, pamphlets and articles, ranging from technical analyses to popular features, and covering legal, social and educational background. Primarily designed as a resource for police training courses, this sampling has also proved to be a valuable tool for intergroup workers, public officials, jurists, citizens' committees and civic leaders.   **25¢**

INSTITUTE OF HUMAN RELATIONS PRESS • 165 East 56 Street, New York, N.Y. 10022

HERBERT T. JENKINS, Chief of Police, Atlanta: Only a man who has been intimately involved with law enforcement could have written this much-needed analysis of police problems, minority-group grievances and the steps needed to end the bitterness between the police and the community.

SENATOR ROBERT F. KENNEDY: A small volume rich in the insight it offers, and the proposals it makes. . . . Judge Edwards knows that until the police and the urban communities they serve regard one another as allies in a common cause, the tensions and difficulties will remain, to threaten the peace of our cities.

SENATOR THOMAS H. KUCHEL: . . . a cogent analysis of the misunderstandings that so often separate the police from minority-group communities and the broader problems of law enforcement in an urban society. Community leaders and citizens throughout America would do well to follow his advice.

HOWARD R. LEARY, Police Commissioner, New York City: There is no question that it is a modern basic text in police-community relations . . . Informative, instructive, a set of guidelines with objectives and goals clearly spelled out.

BAYARD RUSTIN, Executive Director, A. Philip Randolph Institute: As an ex-police commissioner, Judge George Edwards is well qualified to discuss the extremely critical relationship between the police and Negro communities. His pamphlet should make a valuable contribution to the understanding and, hopefully, solution of Negro and police conflict.

CARL B. STOKES, Mayor of Cleveland: The police-community relationship has become the most vital link in urban living. *The Police on the Urban Frontier* provides a genuine and intelligent insight into the pressures and problems and the policeman's participation. It should be read by all persons in law enforcement at any level.

MARVIN E. WOLFGANG, Chairman, Department of Sociology, University of Pennsylvania: This booklet pulls together some of the most perceptive thoughts and cogent factual evidence available on the police and their critical role in our modern urban society. I know of no single document that speaks as eloquently and clearly to so large an audience as this one.

Institute of Human Relations Press, 165 East 56 St., New York, N. Y. 10022